D0269417

HOME BREWING –
THE CAMRA GUIDE

Graham Wheeler

*'There is one other agreeable consequence. Under the present
law, people who brew beer either for their own consumption
or, in the case of farmers, for consumption by their work
people, are required to take out an excise licence and, in some
cases to pay duty based on the Schedule A valuation. The
amount of revenue involved is very small indeed, and is
probably less than the cost of collection. The abolition of the
Schedule A valuation system provides a convenient opportunity
for getting rid of these licences. So the private citizen will
have the same freedom to brew beer as he already has to
make wine.'*

Reginald Maudling, Budget April 3rd 1963.

Home Brewing

THE
CAMRA
GUIDE

Graham Wheeler

Illustrations by Kate Mahaffey

ALMA
BOOKS

Author: **Graham Wheeler**
Design: **Opus Design Group**
Illustrations: **Kate Mahaffey**

Typeset and printed by: **Cambridge University Press**
ISBN **1–85249–107–8**
Published by **Alma Books Ltd.,** a wholly owned
subsidiary of the campaign for Real Ale., Alma Road,
St Albans, Herts.

Thanks to McMullen & Co of Hertford who allowed
Kate Mahaffey to sketch in their Brewery

Introduction

"Before I proceed to give any directions about brewing, let me mention some of the inducements to do the thing. In former times, to set about to show to Englishmen that it was good for them to brew beer in their own houses, would have been as impertinent as gravely to insist that they ought to endeavour not to lose their breath; for in those times (only forty years ago), to have a house and not to brew was a very rare thing indeed." (William Cobbett, COTTAGE ECONOMY, 1821.)

The CAMRA Home Brewing Guide is intended to act as a *standard* reference work for the discerning home brewer, novice or experienced, who wishes to be able to brew high-quality, full-flavoured, traditional style ales at home. It is intended to be the definitive reference work for the home brewer and bridge the gap between amateur and professional brewing. I have tried to cover every aspect of brewing to considerable depth, but in terms that anyone can understand.

It is not necessary to have a master's degree in biotechnology to understand the brewing process or to be able to brew quality ale at home which equals or surpasses many commercially-made counterparts. There is no need whatsoever for home brewed ales to be cloudy, have off-tastes and tangs, induce disproportionate hangovers, or indeed be too weak or too strong. This book should show you how to produce ales that are a pleasure to brew, a pleasure to drink, and which can be offered to your visitors with pride.

Commercially brewed beer is slowly changing character, and the distinction between various brewers' products is gradually disappearing. This is part of a quest, on the part of some national brewers, to make certain beers appeal to a wider consumer base without the need of the potential new customer to "acquire the taste". As one CAMRA wag once pointed out, one way of achieving this aim is to remove the taste – at least that way no one will find the taste offensive! I can see the day dawning when all British beer will taste the same, as, in my opinion, most keg bitters and lagers taste the same. The brewing of genuine, full-flavoured beers may, one day, become a cottage craft, with traditional methods being propagated by a loyal band of ardent home brewers. Already we have the near extinction of proper brown ale and proper mild ale, and only a few breweries produce a genuine old ale or a winter brew. Traditional bitter itself nearly faded into obscurity in the early seventies, and may well have done so, had it not been for the efforts of CAMRA members. Home brewing enables us to produce any type of beer that we please without the restrictions imposed by commercial considerations.

One does not write a book of this nature without a great deal of help from the established brewing industry. I would particularly like to thank the following organisations for their help: ABM Ltd, The Bass Museum, English Hops Ltd, Munton and Fison plc, Pauls Malt Ltd, and Lupofresh.

I would also like to thank C.F.G., who not only presented me with C. L. Duddington's excellent book, "Plain Man's Guide to Beer", the book which sparked off my passion for our brewing heritage, but who also made an off-the-cuff remark which first inspired me to put pen to paper on this Magnum Opus.

Wassail!

Graham Wheeler

High Wycombe September 1990

Contents

ALL
YOUR OWN
WORK.

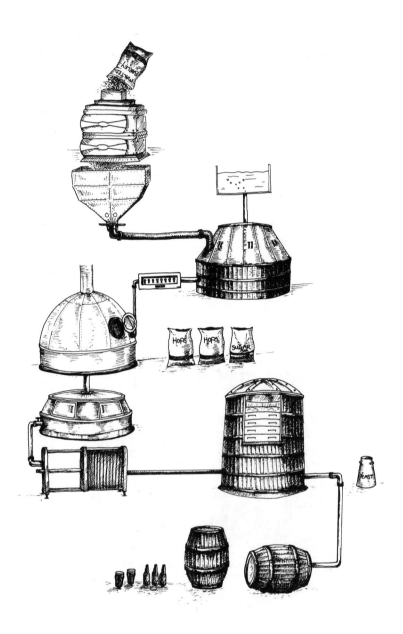

The commercial brewing process

1 The rise of commercial brewing

'They (the working man) still drink beer, but in general, it is of the brewing of common brewers, and in public-houses, of which the common brewers have become the owners, and have thus, by the aid of paper money, obtained a monopoly in the supplying of the great body of the people with one of those things which, to the hard-working man, is almost a necessary of life. These things must be altered or the nation must be sunk into nothingness.'
(William Cobbett, 1821)

The origins of commercial brewing in this country can be reliably traced back to the middle ages when monasteries would offer travellers accommodation and refreshment. The refreshment included ale, which was brewed by the monks themselves. The monks, who presumably had plenty of time on their hands, were able to put considerable effort into their brewing activities and as a consequence acquired considerable skill in the production of ale. No doubt the monks also sold their ale wholesale to local hostelries, the households of local nobility, and to ship's masters if the monastery was situated close to a port.

When Henry VIII dissolved the monasteries a number of brewer monks suddenly found themselves unemployed. It was these monks who probably set the foundation for the common brewer (wholesale brewer) in this country. Upon dissolution the estates and property of the monasteries, which would have included brewhouses and malthouses, were usually passed on to local nobility. It is logical to assume that the redundant monks would use their superior brewing skills to their advantage, and would either become brewers for the new owners of their property, or would set up breweries on their own account to produce ale for their previous customers. Usually the local nobility employed the monks to continue brewing on their behalf, and apart from making ale for the household, also sold the ale to the tenants of their huge estates, which, incidentally, gives us the tradition of addressing a publican as Landlord. However, despite the activities of these redundant monks, the common brewer was a rare beast for as long as one hundred years after the dissolution.

At the turn of the eighteenth century there were quite a number of common brewers in London where the explosive growth of the city and the sheer size of the rapidly expanding market enabled them to eke out a living. However, the impact of these pioneering common brewers on the London beer market was quite insignificant, they were small businesses by any standard and their growth was noticeably unspectacular. By and large, the common brewers were unable to persuade the publican to relinquish brewing and to purchase his ale from them.

However, after two hundred years of insignificance, the fortunes of the London common brewer was about to change with the advent of 'Entire'!

Entire

It became customary for the Londoners of the early 1700's to drink a mixture of three different beers, a concoction known as 'Three Threads', in much the same way as twentieth century drinkers mix mild and bitter. One enterprising brewer had the idea of brewing a beer with the same qualities as 'three threads' but contained entirely in one cask. He called it 'Entire Butt'. It was a strong dark beer and it was an immediate success. Ralf Harwood the brewer concerned, was also astute enough to demonstrate the earliest recorded example of commercial market dumping! He priced 'Entire Butt' to undercut almost every other type of beer on the market, although in reality it was an expensive beer to produce. Other common brewers followed Ralf Harwood's example, and 'Entire', or 'Porter', as the drink became to be known, took the City by storm.

At last the London common brewers had done it! They had actively encouraged, nay – damn near created, a demand for a product in which the publican brewers could not compete. Even if the publican brewers knew how to brew the new drink, it apparently took well over a year to mature, and there were not many publicans who could afford to lay down a years supply of beer in advance. Economies of scale soon maintained the price of Entire well below anything that the publicans could brew. The age of the common brewer had dawned, and publican brewing in London died almost overnight. By about 1750 the London porter brewers were some of the wealthiest men in the country.

The provincial common brewer

Despite the spectacular rise of the London common brewer, outside of London common brewing was almost unheard of, even as late as 1750. Although it is recorded that Mary Queen of Scots, during the sixteenth century, smuggled secret messages out of prison in the empty barrels of a Burton brewer, and a survey of 1727 stated that: 'The clear and dry Burton, Litchfield, and Derby ales, Yorkshire stingo, Doncaster, and Nottingham ale, Norwich nogg, Plymouth white ale, Newbury beer, and West Country twankam were sold in London'; it is unlikely that the sale of ale from country breweries was very extensive. In his book, 'The English Alehouse', Peter Clark states that in 1725, over a 1,000 barrels of ale a year were being shipped from Burton via Hull, to London. However, 1,000 barrels a year is an insignificant quantity when one considers that a single medium sized modern pub will sell around 500 barrels a year.

It was not until about 1770 that the country common brewer began to appear in any number, possibly encouraged by the publication of the first scientific treatise on brewing by Michael Combrune in the late 1760's which exposed many of the hitherto closely guarded secrets of the successful London brewers. Provincial breweries began to spring up in areas of highest growth and prosperity; such as the coaching towns along the trade routes into London and the young industrial revolution towns of the Midlands. Initially business for the provincial common brewer was very sluggish as it was for the London brewers more than seventy years before. There were many reasons for this, not least the fact that their potential market size was tiny compared to the London brewers' market. 'Porter' or 'Entire' was particularly a London phenomenon; it did not really catch on in the provinces. Country folk preferred the more conventional ales. Some of the more fortunate common brewers got an unexpected boost when thousands of 'navvies' descended upon an area to build a stretch of canal. This caused demand to outstrip the publicans' brewing capacity for a few years, forcing them to buy from the common brewer.

At the turn of the nineteenth century things had not improved much. A country publican was still not prepared to buy from a brewery a product which he had been making himself for years. This is not surprising, because in the countryside brewing was as much a part of running a home as were washing, cooking, and baking. A country person would find it unthinkable to go out and buy ready made ale, in the same way that you and I would not go to the supermarket and buy five gallons of ready made tea! The publicans had the same view; malt and time were readily available in the countryside; why should they buy something from a brewer when the 'missus' would make it for nothing? Unlike the London brewer, the country brewer did not have a product that could persuade, or force the publicans to relinquish brewing.

The first major inroads that the common brewers would have made into the established trade would probably have been in the supply of summer beer. Good beer could not be brewed during the summer due to the higher ambient temperatures and the inevitable infection from airborne spoilage organisms; which are much more abundant during the summer months. Summer brewed beer did not keep, and in very warm weather it was often sour before it had finished brewing. The common brewers overcame this problem by brewing the whole summer's supply of ale during the winter brewing season, which ran from October through to the end of May, and storing it until summer. Putting down an adequate supply of ale for the summer was no problem for the common brewer with his greater resources; but it was a different matter for the publican brewer, who did not have the same resources. This often led to the situation that, during the summer at least, ale from the common brewers was of higher quality than the publicans' summer brewed ale.

The provincial common brewer soon began to realise that the best way of expanding his business was firstly to produce an ale with an agreeable flavour, and thereafter provide a level of quality and consistency which the publican brewer was unable to maintain. This probably was not very difficult to achieve, one can appreciate that there must have been some pretty ghastly stuff on sale! The common brewers were much better equipped than their publican counterparts and considered themselves to be part of the scientific community. Many were ardent experimenters and put a considerable amount of time and effort into trying to improve the quality, economy, and, therefore, the saleability of their products. In the early 19th century efficient steam heating of the coppers was introduced, steam sterilisation was introduced, mashing techniques were improved, the dropping system was devised, and the 'big daddy' of them all, cooling techniques or **attemperation** was introduced.

By pumping cold water through pipes submerged in the cooling trays, and in the fermenting vessels, brewers were able to control temperatures sufficiently to enable some brewing to take place during the summer months. The ability of the common brewers to brew during the summer, or at least extend their brewing season somewhat, gave them an incalculable advantage in both efficiency and the ability to meet unexpected demand. Even with cooling techniques, summer brewed ale still did not possess the keeping qualities of winter brewed ale, but it kept a lot better than was previously possible. Summer brewing was confined to brewing beer for immediate local consumption, and to brewing the old winter ales where the higher alcohol and hop content kept infecting organisms quiet. It was still common practice to brew most of the summer's supply of ale during the winter season and store it. In fact, brewing remained largely seasonal right up to the middle of the present century.

By about 1825 the common brewer had only gained about 30% of the total beer market, but it is fair to assume that the great majority of this percentage was contributed by the huge London porter brewers, who, by this time time, had gained 95% of the massive London market. The London porter brewers had been thriving and expanding for around one hundred years, whereas the provincial common brewer was still fighting for existence. Many of the provincial common brewers had been in business for over forty years and they had hardly managed to scratch the surface of their potential market. However, change was on the way!

Although the provincial brewers were expanding painfully slowly, nevertheless they **were** expanding. This expansion was providing the brewers with increased resources and considerable brewing experience. It was this experience and resources that would ultimately provide the more skilful common brewers with their future. There was still one further 19th century development that was to put the stamp of fortune on the provincial brewers. .... Snobbery !.

The birth of Pale Ale

London's immensely popular, strong, dark drink, 'Porter' or 'Entire', had, by now, been around for about one hundred years, and had attracted a working class stigma. A stigma that is still attached to dark beers to this very day! The middle classes distinguished themselves by drinking the more expensive lighter coloured beers, wines, or spirits. A middle class gentleman would not be seen dead with a glass of Porter in his hand! In those days, all beers were considerably darker than they are today, and probably fairly cloudy. In view of this, another enterprising London brewer had the idea of brewing a very light coloured, clean looking beer, designed to appeal to the middle classes. Pale Ale was born, and it was an immediate success. The provincial brewers took to brewing pale ale and it was soon discovered that their higher brewing skills enabled them to brew better, clearer pale ale than the London brewers. who, unlike the provincial brewer had spent the last hundred years brewing a very dark, Guinness-like beer. Furthermore certain breweries were geographically located where the water supply was better suited to the brewing of pale ale than was London water, notably Burton upon Trent and certain areas of the Chilterns.

At last the provincial breweries were on the map! They now had a product with which the publicans and even the huge London porter brewers could not compete in terms of quality and clarity. Snobbery did the rest! Pale ale swept the country and eventually the world, inverse snobbery created a secondary demand for 'Entire' in the provinces, giving the provincial brewers the best of both worlds. From this point on publican brewing declined rapidly and the common brewers expanded just as rapidly in their respective areas. The demand for pale ale was overwhelming and regional breweries sprang up all over the country to supply the new beer. Now it was the provincial brewers' turn to became some of the richest and most influential men in their community, and their breweries to become some of the most scientifically advanced industrial establishments in the world.

Undoubtably brewing's golden years were the period from about 1840 to about 1870. During the 1850's more pubs were opened than at any other time in brewing history, and many new breweries were started. This was brought about by the increased mobility that railways gave to industry. Britain's industry was booming, business men were travelling around the country, people were moving from the countryside into the towns for higher paid work, and industrial towns were rapidly expanding to cope. Pubs sprang up wherever there were travellers or workers, and there were lots of both. Full employment and social revolution led to higher paid work, which gave people increased disposable income. More and more publican brewers began to buy their ale from the common brewers because they were unable to brew the increasingly popular Pale Ale, either as well, or as cheaply as could the common brewers.

Even the most skilful brewers could only expand as far as the cumbersome means of transport would permit. The sphere of influence of any one brewer was often limited to about a 15 mile radius of the brewery. A comfortable days limit for a horse drawn dray. If a brewery wished to expand outside his particular area, he needed a method of moving his beer in bulk. Horse drawn road vehicles could not really carry beer in bulk, and the often bumpy ride could cause the pressure within the barrels to reach bursting point, particularly in hot weather. The expansion of many otherwise excellent breweries was abruptly halted once they had reached the boundaries imposed by the limitations of the transport available to them. On the other hand, certain breweries were favoured with rivers or canals, or the building of a main railway line through their home town. The railways gave these fortunate breweries the ability to transport their product directly into London or other rapidly expanding towns of the industrial revolution. To appreciate the role that transport played in the rise of the breweries it is appropriate to consider the fortunes of the breweries of Burton upon Trent, the Bass brewery in particular, because it still survives to tell its story:

Almost from day one the Brewers of Burton upon Trent had all the ingredients for success. They had a considerable brewing heritage which dated back to the Benedictine monks who founded Burton Abbey in 1002 AD, and who were certainly brewing in 1295 AD. In short there have always been breweries in Burton upon Trent. When Pale ale burst onto the market in about 1825, not only was Burton already an established brewing centre, but the already respected Burton brewers had the River Trent and the Trent and Mersey canal, which gave them easy access to the up and coming towns of the industrial revolution, Derby, Birmingham, Leicester, Manchester, Liverpool, and Hull. The coming of the Midland Railway in 1839 gave them the ability to transport their beer directly into London and to other parts of the country.

Bass began brewing in 1777, but sixty years later in 1837 the total output from the brewery amounted to only 10,000 barrels per annum. Ten years later in 1847, eight years after the coming of the Midland railway, the output had increased to about 60,000 barrels per annum, and during this period the brewery was considerably enlarged to cope. By 1853, only six years later, the output of the brewery had increased to 130,000 barrels and a second brewery was built. Again only ten years later in 1863 the output had increased to 400,000 barrels per annum and a third brewery was erected. By 1876 the output had reached 900,000 barrels per annum and the first brewery was pulled down and rebuilt on a much larger scale.

The growth of the Bass brewery was no doubt exceptional, but all of the good pale ale breweries demonstrated rapid growth during this period, if not quite as spectacular. At one time Reading and Newbury boasted 27 breweries between them, and Burton upon Trent had as many as 40 at any one time. The major reason that Burton grew to be the largest brewing centre in the country is that it is centrally located with a radiating network of rivers, canals, and railways; enabling beer to be transported quickly and cheaply to anywhere in the country. The water quality of Burton upon Trent was really of secondary importance.

The name of Burton upon Trent is synonymous with that of Bass, even though there were some 40 other breweries in the town. By consistent quality and entrepreneurial flair the Bass brewery grew to be the largest brewery in the world.

Their beers were available all over England and in many parts of the globe. The size of the Bass brewery, before the turn of this century, was awe inspiring. The brewery, malt houses, offices, stables, coopers, ale stores, etc. covered an area of 755 acres! The brewery contained 29 coppers, several hundred fermenting vessels, and it brewed close to one million gallons a week! The brewery had 11 private railway engines and about 12 miles of private railway around its premises. It needed the services of around 500 railway wagons per day to transport the beer. Its London ale depot held 160,000 casks of beer, and, at the brewery, it was a common sight to see a quarter of a million casks of beer maturing in the open air, stacked in great pyramids. The Bass brewery would not have reached this immense size if it were not for its reputation for quality and for the excellent communications that the area afforded. Despite its immense size, the Bass brewery produced only 4.5% of Britain's beer production, and Burton upon Trent, in total, probably only accounted for something like 7%. There was still something like twenty million gallons a week being brewed by the other common brewers around the country.

By 1880 beer was Britain's second largest industry, second only to cotton, and British beer was highly sought after all over the world. From about 1900 onwards the consumption of beer per capita began to decline, but that's an entirely different story.

2 Traditional commercial brewing

Brewers have from tuns and coolers,
Arose to be our sovereign rulers,
And still to their immortal praise,
Build coaches daily out of drays.
(About 1714, From THE ENGLISH ALEHOUSE, Peter Clark 1983)

Traditional malting

The primary ingredient of English beer is malted barley. In days long past, all breweries malted their own barley, and this was performed in a traditional floor maltings. Harvest time was an extremely busy period for the maltsters because a whole season's supply of barley would begin to arrive from the local farmers in a seemingly never ending stream. The barley had to be malted as soon as possible after harvesting because the grain would rapidly deteriorate during storage, particularly if it was damp. If damp, the grain would continue to respire during storage causing destructive temperatures to be developed in the centre of the bulk, whereas in the cooler regions partial germination may take place thereby ruining its brewing properties. Furthermore, any pests collected with the harvest would continue to attack the grain. However, the barley arrived in too great a volume to be malted immediately.

The maltster's first task was to partially dry the grain as it arrived and put it into temporary storage in readiness for malting. Drying was performed by spreading the grain onto the malting floors and opening ventilators in the side of the building. This caused an air flow across the surface of the grain. The grain was turned over frequently to ensure even drying. Drying retarded respiration and eliminated the possibility of mildew. Successful long term storage of barley for brewing purposes requires that the moisture content of the grain be between certain limits. This was difficult to estimate, and besides, with floor drying and manual turning it was well nigh impossible to ensure uniform moisture content throughout the bulk. To be safe, the maltsters of yesteryear were forced to malt the barley as soon as was practical, and as soon as the grain was safely in store, the malting season began in earnest.

Before the malting of a quantity of barley was begun it was first graded by means of '**Boby's screens**', so named after the man who devised the first automatic grading machines. These were nothing more earth shattering than a series of mechanically actuated sieves. The screens had the effect of removing stones, leaves, and other debris, and performed the important task of grading the grain into its various sizes. A uniform grain size is important because the maltster requires that all of the grain in any one batch should germinate at the same rate.

After the screening operation the grain was stored in garners, which were large storage boxes situated on an upper floor above the steeping tanks. The steeping tanks were known as cisterns or steeps.

At the start of malting a batch of barley, trap-doors were opened in the storage garners and a quantity of grain was allowed to flow into the cistern. The grain was steeped in the cistern until it had absorbed enough water to begin germination. During the steep the water was changed several times, partly to wash the grain clean, but primarily to ensure that the water contained an adequate supply of dissolved oxygen for the germination process. After the grain had taken on water it was removed from the cistern and spread out on to the growing floor of the maltings to continue with the germination. The process of germination caused heat to be evolved and the grain was maintained at about 15°C by varying the depth of the grain on the floor. If it was too hot it was spread out further across the floor, or heaped up more thickly if it was too cold. The grain was frequently turned over by the maltsters to maintain a constant temperature throughout the bulk, thereby ensuring even germination. During germination rootlets sprout from the barley, and germination was deemed to have proceeded far enough when these rootlets had grown to a particular length. Towards the end of the germination phase the grain was piled high in order to increase the temperature of the bulk to about 22°C. It was turned rather more frequently and ventilators were opened close to the floor of the malt house which caused an air flow across the surface of the grain. This partially dried the **green malt** and arrested germination in preparation for the kilning phase.

The point at which germination is stopped varies according to the type of malt being produced. A malt is known as well modified if germination has been allowed to proceed for a long period, and poorly modified or partially modified if germination is stopped after a short period of time. English brewing favours the use of well modified malts, whereas Continental practice traditionally favoured the use of poorly modified malts. Poorly modified malts require the use of the Continental decoction mash process during brewing in order to complete the modification and to reduce the nitrogen/protein content of the malt to acceptable limits.

Kilning the malt

After the germination phase of the malt, the malt then enters the kilning phase of its production. The kilning phase dries the malt which arrests germination completely and colours the malt. Different degrees of kilning produces different coloured malts with correspondingly different flavours. The range of malts vary from pale malt, which is the staple ingredient of all English beers, through amber and brown malts to black malt which is roasted almost to complete destruction.

There are some active floor maltings still in existence, but they are very rare.

These days the majority of brewing malt is made, not by the breweries, but by the large commercial maltsters who employ modern techniques and automation to enable them to process large volumes of barley very quickly and economically. There are several 'scientific' acceleration techniques that can be applied to considerably speed up the malting process, such as gibberellic acid treatment. I suspect that modern malting technique may leave a lot to be desired as to the brewing qualities of the malt thus produced, but it is not difficult to understand why the breweries have abandoned their maltings in favour of the white coated, high speed, push button, mass producers.

At the turn of this century, Bass had three breweries at Burton upon Trent. To supply these breweries with malt, Bass also owned a total of 42 malting houses, the buildings of which covered a combined area in excess of some 400 acres! These maltings required the services of some 450 semi-skilled men for about four months of the year (the malting season). It is obvious that malting was not only very expensive in both labour and property, but with the rushed nature of the malting season, and the temporary hiring of a substantial number of semi-skilled men, it was also quite an extensive logistics problem for the breweries. Incidently, the temporary maltsters were usually farm workers, who in those days, invariably, found themselves redundant from the harvest until the next spring.

In the brewery

The shape, size and layout of traditional breweries vary tremendously, depending upon their capacity, the traditions and technology of the time that they were built, and the extent of alterations and enlargements made over the years. They range from the gigantic five storey factory type buildings typical of the large brewers of London and Burton upon Trent, which from the outside are not much different in appearance to any other large 19th century factory; to the quaint Victorian tower breweries which were typical of the smaller country brewers.

Before the malt can be used for brewing it must first be cracked or milled. This is normally performed by passing the malt between two or more sets of steel rollers, rather like an old fashioned washing mangle. The cracking of the malt fractures the grain to enable the water in the subsequent mashing process to reach the starches contained within the malt. Cracking of the malt is not normally performed until it is ready to be used for a brew, because should the malt become even slightly damp during storage, it will become **slack** and be unsuitable for brewing. After milling the malt is mixed with the other malts or malt adjuncts used in the recipe and is now called **grist**, it is passed to the grist case where it is held in readiness for mashing. The grist case is often heated and is situated above the **mash tun**.

Water for brewing

The water used for brewing is often drawn from the brewery's own well. It is pumped from the well into storage tanks in readiness for use. There is often a separate water treatment tank where the water is treated to give it a composition appropriate to the type of beer that is being brewed, a process known as Burtonising. Brewers call their brewing water **liquor** to distinguish it from the water used for washing etc. The relative mineral content of the liquor affects the subsequent mash and has an important bearing on the outcome of the final product, different water compositions favour different types of beer.

The mash

Mashing is the process of extracting fermentable sugars from the grist by steeping it in hot water for about two hours. The operation being performed in a vessel known as a **mash tun**. During the mash, enzymes contained in the malt convert the starches into fermentable sugars, a reaction known as **saccharification**. The enzymes responsible for saccharification are very temperature sensitive, and therefore the temperature of the mash must be maintained as closely as possible to its ideal of about 66°C. If the mashing temperature is too high, the enzymes responsible for conversion may be destroyed, whereas if the temperature is too low an inefficient mash may result. The temperature of the mash must be maintained within about 3°C throughout the two hour mashing period. The brewers relied upon good thermal insulation of the mash tun to prevent excessive heat loss during the mashing period.

The English mash tun that has evolved over the years is a large cylindrical vessel which is usually unheated, but nevertheless, well insulated. It is fitted with an insulated cover and is often fitted with rotating mechanical stirrers known as **Armstrong rakes** or **porcupines**. These serve to mix the grist into a thick mushy paste and ensure that there are no dry pockets.

Obviously, the action of mixing the cool grist with the hot liquor lowers the temperature of the overall mash somewhat. The ideal starting temperature of the mash is around 66°C (**initial heat**), but the grist needs to be introduced to liquor which is at a higher temperature, about 75°C, known as **strike heat**, to compensate for the drop. If the strike heat is too high some of the conversion enzymes in the malt may be destroyed, and yet if the initial heat is too low an inefficient mash may result. Some breweries ease this problem by heating the grist prior to its introduction to the liquor. In these breweries the grist case (the hopper above the mash tun which holds the grist in readiness) is heated to reduce the important temperature differential between strike heat and initial heat; this allows the use of a lower strike heat, and consequently reduces the potential for errors.

At the start of a brew a quantity of hot brewing liquor is run into the mash tun. When the liquor in the mash tun has cooled to **strike heat** the grist from the grist case is allowed to flow into the mash tun, and the porcupines are set in motion and allowed to run for two or three revolutions, after which they are turned off. In some breweries the grist is pre-mixed with the mash liquor before entry to the mash tun using a device called a **Steele's pre-masher**. This is an archimedean screw affair enclosed in a tube, the grist case being at one end, and the whole contraption is mounted above the mash tun. The grist is carried to the mash tun by means of the archimedean screw, but about half way along it meets a flow of mash liquor maintained at an appropriate strike heat. The Steele's masher has the effect of ensuring that the grist is well mixed with the liquor, avoiding dry spots, and eliminating the need for Armstrong rakes, although they are usually also fitted. The pre-masher also helps to reduce the critical difference between strike heat and initial heat.

When the grist and liquor have been introduced to the mash tun and well mixed, the porcupines are turned off and the mash is allowed to stand for one-and-a-half to two hours. If the temperature of the mash falls too much it can be raised by running some more hot liquor into the bottom of the mash tun, a process known as **underletting**. When the mash has proceeded far enough, the process is often halted by raising the temperature to about 77°C. This is done because the subsequent running and sparging operation is a slow one, and can take two hours or more. If the process was not halted saccharification would continue until the boiling phase, with the result that the grain would be over mashed. The temperature is usually raised by underletting, but this has the danger of diluting the wort too much. A more modern method is to run off some of the wort and return it to the mash tun via a heat exchanger.

When the mash is complete, taps are opened in the bottom of the tun and the sweet wort is allowed to run off into a receptacle known as a **spendsafe.** The goods in the mash tun settle down onto a mesh that covers the bottom of the tun. The goods act as a filter bed for the wort, which removes solid particles and debris. The first runnings from the mash tun are usually turbid and are returned to the mash tun until the **sweet wort** 'runs bright', at which point it is directed to the **underback**. The underback is a heated holding tank which collects the sweet wort in readiness for the boiling phase. The wort must not be allowed to cool before the boiling phase otherwise off-tastes and hazes may be produced in the finished beer. When the sweet wort has been run off, the goods in the mash tun still retain much of the sugary matter, and this must be flushed out – a process known as **sparging**. The mash tun is equipped with rotating perforated pipes known as **sparge arms**. These operate in much the same way as a domestic lawn sprinkler and gently spray hot water, at about 77°C, onto the grains to flush out the remaining sugars. The specific gravity of the spargings is monitored and sparging is halted when this falls below about 1005. Over sparging extracts undesirable substances from the grains which cause off-tastes and hazes, apart from the risk of over diluting the wort. The sweet wort is then directed to the **copper** for the boiling phase.

The boil

During boiling, bacteria contained in the wort is destroyed, haze forming proteins are precipitated out of solution, undesirable volatile substances are driven off, and a series of complicated chemical reactions take place, all of which affect the quality of the final product.

At the onset of boiling any brewing sugars used in the recipe are added to the copper, and when the boil is well under way, about three quarters of the hops are added. During the boil some of the flavour and aroma giving substances of the hops are distilled off, therefore about twenty five percent of the hops are often held back until the last fifteen minutes of the boil. **Copper finings** are often added towards the end of the boil, this is usually **carragheen**, commonly known as **Irish moss**, but is in fact a seaweed. This helps to coagulate the proteins in the wort and assist in their precipitation out of solution.

Traditionally the copper was heated by coal or coke, but from early Victorian times onwards this was gradually replaced by superheated steam. The very first recorded use of steam for any manufacturing process was devised by the incredible Joseph Bramah, and installed in Hartford's London brewery in 1785! A very vigorous boil is desirable in order to drive off the unwanted volatile products. This not only consumes a considerable amount of energy but also runs the risk of darkening the wort too much. Most coppers are equipped with a passive device, known as a **calandria**, which behaves very much like a coffee percolator and keeps the wort circulating within the copper. This helps to drive off the volatile substances, and considerably reduces the amount of energy required to perform the boil.

Cooling

When the boiling phase is complete the wort is run from the copper into a receptacle called the **hopback**, this removes the spent hops from the wort, the hops settle on the bottom of the vessel and act as a filter bed which filters the **trub** (precipitated protein matter) out of the wort. The wort must then be rapidly cooled to pitching temperature. This not only helps to keep bacterial infection at bay, but also forces further precipitation of protein matter out of solution. Cooling was traditionally performed by very large flat open cooling trays situated at the top of the brewery, the cooling being performed by the simple means of atmospheric evaporation. Later the cooling was assisted by passing cold water through pipes situated in the trays, and eventually this was used in conjunction with a device which brewers called a **refrigerator** in which the wort was allowed to trickle, like a waterfall, over a series of pipes through which cold water was pumped. A more modern form of cooler is a heat exchanger, usually referred to as a **paraflow,** in which the wort meets a counter current of cold water, separated from it by means of very thin copper, or stainless steel baffle plates.

Once the wort has been cooled it may be left to stand for a while to allow more trub to settle, or the trub may be removed by means of a **whirlpool**, a circular chamber that sets up a cyclone in the wort which removes the trub by drawing it into the eye of the whirlpool.

The boiling phase of beer production drives off the dissolved oxygen in the wort, but the yeast needs oxygen during the initial aerobic growth phase prior to alcoholic fermentation. Open trough coolers absorb some air through the exposed surface of the wort, and refrigerators absorb copious amounts of air due to their waterfall action. Paraflows are totally enclosed. The wort is not given the opportunity to absorb air, and therefore air needs to be introduced into the wort by some other method. In some breweries air is introduced into the wort at the time of filling the fermentation vessel by spraying the wort through roses (called **tunners**), thereby admitting atmospheric oxygen. Other breweries blow filtered air into the fermentation vessel, or into the cold end of the paraflow.

Fermentation

The wort is directed from the cooler to the fermentation vessel. Here the volume and temperature of the wort are adjusted by adding hot or cold liquor as appropriate. The yeast is then added (**pitched**) and the volume and specific gravity of the wort are measured and recorded for excise purposes.

The temperature at which fermentation is conducted is obviously important. The process of fermentation causes heat to be generated which could raise the temperature of the wort above acceptable limits and cause off-tastes to be produced in the beer. The temperature of the fermentation vessel is controlled by means of **attemperators**. These are coils of piping set round the inside of the fermentation vessel, through which hot or cold water can be pumped to maintain the temperature of the wort between the normal limits of 16°C and 20°C.

Some breweries ferment down in a single fermentation vessel, but others utilise the **dropping system** whereby the fermentation is started in one vessel, but when it has gone about half way it is carefully 'dropped' into another vessel, usually situated on the floor below, where fermentation is completed. The dropping system undoubtably produces more stable beer. The beer produced by the breweries that practice the method is usually highly regarded for its quality and flavour. Unfortunately the dropping system is not economical as regards vessel utilisation and is slowly becoming extinct. There are several variations upon the basic dropping system, the most famous of which is the Burton Union System, which was used by the brewers of Burton Upon Trent.

In the Burton Union method of brewing, fermentation was started in conventional open fermentation **squares**, but when fermentation had gone about half way it was dropped into the **unions** situated on the floor below. Each union was a series of about sixteen carriage casks arranged in two rows, each cask held 144 gallons. A vertical **swan neck** pipe rose out of the shive of each cask. The gas generated by fermentation caused yeast to be forced up the swan neck pipe, which then fell into the **balm trough**. The balm trough was situated above and between the two rows of casks. The wort forced up with the yeast ran back into the casks via a union pipe which connected the balm trough and all the casks together via the bung holes, the yeast remained behind in the trough from where it could be removed. Towards the end of fermentation the balm trough was maintained at a lower temperature than the casks to facilitate the sedimentation of the yeast. The Burton Union system caused the yeast and wort to continually circulate, resulting in a characteristic flavour. Surplus yeast was easy to remove thereby reducing the danger of dead cells causing off-tastes. At the end of fermentation the yeast was in the trough, leaving comparatively clear beer in the casks. I suspect that the union system of brewing was as much responsible for the fame of Burton brewed beers, as was any other factor. Alas, due to the high cost of maintenance, the system is almost extinct. At the turn of the century, the various union rooms at the Bass brewery contained a total of 4,590 of these 144 gallon casks.

Back to the fermentation process. During fermentation the the heavy sugars in the wort are converted to lighter alcohol, causing the specific gravity of the wort to progressively fall. This fall in specific gravity is called wort **attenuation.** When the wort has attenuated to **racking gravity** the fermentation is stopped by pumping cold water through the attemperators and lowering the temperature. The fermentation is stopped at this stage to ensure that there is sufficient fermentable material remaining in the wort to promote a **secondary fermentation** in the barrels during the maturing stage. The cooling also has the beneficial effect of causing most of the remaining yeast to sediment out. Some breweries allow fermentation to proceed to final gravity before **racking**, in which case priming sugar or a quantity of actively fermenting wort must be added to the barrels to promote the secondary fermentation.

Maturation and barrelling

After fermentation, the beer needs time to mature before it is ready to drink. Ordinary beers are usually transferred directly to barrels and the beer is allowed to mature in the barrel. Strong beers, and winter ales, which require a longer maturation time, and beers destined for bottling, are often partially matured in separate conditioning tanks which makes more economical use of the expensive stock of barrels, and of valuable storage space. In days of old the conditioning tanks were often specially constructed wooden tanks, or large 144 gallon carriage casks, but in a modern brewery the tanks are obviously constructed from stainless steel.

The beer is eventually transferred from either a fermentation vessel, or from a maturation tank into a racking tank. Here primings are added if required, and the beer is allowed a time to settle before being carefully syphoned into the barrels. A small quantity of hops is often added to the barrel to give the beer extra flavour and aroma, a technique known as **dry hopping**. The beer is then placed into storage to mature. Maturation can take anything from about ten days for an ordinary bitter, to several months for an old ale. Just before delivery to the pub a quantity of **isinglass** finings are usually added to the barrel to assist in clearing the beer.

In the pub

On arrival at the pub the beer can be stored shive upwards until a couple of days before it is needed, at which time it is carefully placed onto the stillage, vented and tapped. It is then left a couple of days in order to allow the secondary fermentation to subside and for the beer to settle. Venting is accomplished by replacing the hard shive with a porous one, thereby allowing excess gas to escape. Once the secondary fermentation has subsided or 'gone quiet' and it has 'fallen bright' it is ready to be served. The soft spile is replaced by a hard spile if the beer is in danger of going flat.

The temperature at which the beer is stored and served is obviously important. The ideal temperature is between 12°C and 15°C. The deep cellar of a traditional pub keeps a fairly constant temperature throughout the year, but problems are often experienced in high summer. In days now almost past, the publicans would keep their beer cool by covering the barrels with wet hop sacks, but many modern pubs are equipped with air conditioned cellars.

3 Home brewing methods

'A quart of ale is dish for a King'
(Shakespeare)

The main ingredient of beer is malted barley, often simply called malt. As home brewers we can either buy the malt as **grain** and brew **fully mashed** beers from this, or we can use **malt extract.** With a **Mashed beer** we produce the fermentable sugars from the raw malted barley, whereas with malt extract that job has been done for us in a factory. The availability of different products gives rise to four main methods of home brewing: **Beer kits, Malt extract, Partial mash, and Full mash**. These four techniques require differing degrees of involvement and equipment, and likewise provide differing degrees of flexibilty and beer quality.

Beer kits

By far the simplest and easiest method of producing home made beer is to use a wet beer kit. All beers produced from kits are fairly similar, the recipes fixed and inflexible. A beer kit is basically a syrup which consists of malt extract, hop extract, and the other ingredients necessary to produce a fairly standard 'Kit' beer. However, this is a home brewing book intended to help you produce your own distinctive beers. It is just as easy for you to formulate your own kit from the basic malt extract plus hops etc; therefore, there will be little mention of beer kits within these pages.

Malt extract brewing

Devising a recipe from the basic malt extract, rather than using a kit provides greater flexibility and much scope for improving ones beers. Many of the limitations imposed by beer kits are removed. Using malt extract removes the need for mashing or water treatment and so makes the production of a beer fairly straight forward. The minimum equipment required is a brewing bin, some form of boiler, and a few low cost auxiliary bits and bobs. Although this book is mainly concerned about mashed beers, I would heartily recommend the novice brewer to begin by brewing from malt extract.

Partial mash

This is a stage further on from malt extract brewing. The main source of fermentable material is still provided by malt extract, but some of the auxilliary ingredients or adjuncts are mashed in a small mash. This technique provides even greater flexibility to the malt extract brewer, and enables him to produce an even wider range of beers.

Full mash

Grain brewing or **mashing** is the only way of producing distinctive quality beers, and the technique gives the brewer complete flexibility over his product. It is the technique that the 'Grand Masters' of home brewing always use, and is really what this book is all about. Instead of using factory manufactured malt extract as our source of fermentable malt sugars, the full mash uses malted barley, and the fermentable sugars are extracted from the the barley using a special vessel called a **mash tun.** Mashing requires more equipment than extract brewing. It also requires more care, attention, and skill. There is more opportunity for a mistake to be made, and it will take about a day to prepare a brew. Nevertheless it is well worth the effort. There is nothing in the world to match the flavour of properly brewed traditional English beer, and there is nothing in the world to match the pride one feels when one first achieves it.

Mash or malt extract ?

The malt extract argument has raged for years, and it will, no doubt, rage for years to come. The devotees of mashed beers claim that malt extract beers have a pronounced after-taste, the famous 'malt extract tang', that it is impossible to produce a full range of beers using extract, and that the full natural flavour of malt becomes lost. On the other hand, malt extract brewers claim that it is impossible to tell the difference between a mashed beer and an extract beer.

It is not my place to try and settle the argument, after all the flavour of beer is a subjective thing, a matter of individual opinion. However, the weight of evidence falls firmly on the side of the grain brewer. There **are** people who **can** distinguish the difference between grain and extract beers, with a high degree of reliability, and there is no doubt that malt extract lacks the full flavour of true malt. The ratio of fermentable to non fermentable sugars is fixed when one uses malt extract, whereas the ratio can be altered if one mashes. Certain adjuncts which alter the flavour and characteristics of the finished beer need to be mashed, and this puts some adjuncts out of reach of the extract brewer. Despite what the malt extract manufacturers may say, malt extract, in general, is **NOT** made in the same way as a brewers wort.

Having said all that, it is possible to produce perfectly good, acceptable beer from malt extract, and if one is brewing a beer which uses a high proportion of other ingredients, such as crystal malt or roast barley, or if one is brewing a very hoppy beer, it would be very difficult to determine whether the beer was mashed or brewed from malt extract, and even if they could – it does not necessarily mean that it is bad beer. As I have said earlier, the quality and taste of a beer is a subjective thing – a matter of individual opinion.

The copper, where hops are added

4 Home brewing equipment

'The vile obscene talk, noise, nonsense and ribaldry discourses together with the fumes of tobacco, belchings and other foul breakings of wind, that are generally found in an ale-room... are enough to make any rational creature amongst them almost ashamed of his being. But all this rude rabble esteem the highest degree of happiness, and run themselves into the greatest straits imaginable to attain it.'
(From A DISSERTATION ON DRUNKENNESS 1727)

Most of us begin home brewing by purchasing or being given a beer kit, and initially, we use kitchen utensils as our basic equipment. As our interest in this absorbing hobby increases we gradually acquire more equipment to enable us to make our beers more easily. Fortunately the essential pieces of equipment are relatively inexpensive, much of the additional equipment possesed by the ardent home brewer serves to make life easier, rather than being essential to producing good quality beers. There is no need to rush out and buy lots of expensive equipment with the idea that it will automatically enable you to make exhibition quality beers. The foremost requirement for a quality beer is knowledge and experience, equipment comes second.

The following pages outline major items of home brewing equipment required by the budding home brewer.

Fermenting vessels

The first and most essential item that any brewer acquires is his fermenting vessel. The selection of a suitable fermenting vessel should be undertaken with some care. In my opinion, the best type of fermenting bin is the tall, narrow, cylindrical variety, not the shallow bucket shaped type. The bucket shaped type has far too great a ratio of surface area over depth. The smaller surface area of the cylindrical type of vessel makes it easier for the yeast to maintain a protective head, particularly towards the end of fermentation. The greater depth of yeast head will make it easier for the brewer to skim off surplus yeast at the end of fermentation. The deeper and narrower the bin the better, the fermentation is faster and more reliable in a deep bin. The bin, ideally, should have a tap fitted, and should be provided with a close fitting snap on lid to enable the bin to be used for secondary fermentation if desired, or for temporarily protecting the beer when primary fermentation has abated. A hole can be drilled in the lid and a grommet inserted to enable a fermentation lock or a thermometer to be fitted. The standard fermentation bin has a number of additional uses apart from fermentation proper, such as holding sparge liquor, collecting spargings, lugging water into the garage/brewery, mashing etc. It is likely that you will eventually acquire several such bins.

Hydrometer

A hydrometer is an essential, but inexpensive, item of equipment which enables us to measure the specific gravity of our wort at various stages during fermentation. This enables a check to be maintained on how fermentation is progressing. There are various types of hydrometer on the market. The typical brewers' open type of glass hydrometer, which is used in conjunction with a trial jar, is the most suitable type for our purposes. It is advisable for the home brewer to have at least two hydrometers, just in case one gets broken during a brewing session.

The density of a fluid is temperature dependant and hydrometers are calibrated for use at one particular temperature, usually 15°C for brewing hydrometers, or 20°C for chemists' types. To find the S.G. of a fluid which is at a different temperature to that for which the hydrometer is calibrated requires the use of a correction table. Correction tables are supplied with the hydrometers, and there is one on page 165.

Thermometer

Another essential item of equipment is a thermometer. There are various types of thermometer available to the home brewer, some are provided with a float so that they can be suspended in the fluid to be measured, others are fairly basic. At least one of your thermometers should be a high accuracy 300mm (12 inch) type to act as a reference against which you can check your smaller thermometers, or make higher accuracy measurements should you desire. Many of the shorter thermometers supplied to the home brew trade are of rather dubious accuracy. Fortunately, for the most part, home brewing does not demand a tremendous accuracy in temperature measurement, and the cheap small thermometers are perfectly adequate for general purpose use. Electronic thermometers are quite inexpensive these days, I have one which I purchased from a electronic component distributor, it is slightly larger than a ball point pen and cost the equivalent of six pints of (retail) best bitter. One expects that these will become more generally available via the home brewing trade in the near future.

Weighing equipment

Accurate quantitative measurement of our brewing ingredients is essential to producing consistent beer. Modern kitchen scales are the tool usually used for the purpose, and are perfectly adequate for the job, except that they are often not large enough to weigh all of the pale malt used in a particular recipe at one time, this is not a serious disadvantage. I have a cheap set of 5kg scales purchased from Woolworths upon which I stand a two gallon brewing bucket and re-zero the scales. This is perfectly adequate for weighing my pale malt, although strong beers require the measurement to be performed in two lots. A major problem is weighing hops, they are light and very voluminous (what a wonderful word!). To weigh hops, ideally one requires a very sensitive set of scales with a large bin, but the two requirements contradict each other. Modern electronic kitchen scales are just sensitive enough to accurately weigh hops. The ones that I have seen have a resolution of 1 gram, so at 60 grams, which is a typical quantity of hops in a five gallon brew, they will give us about 2% accuracy; which is good enough!

Other paraphernalia

You will automatically aquire an overwhelming assortment of bits and bobs, such that one day you will sit back and wonder where on earth they all came from! Useful brewers widgets include; a long handled brewers paddle, long handled wooden spoon, syphoning tubes, taps, airlocks, funnels, measuring jugs, spoons, bottles, crown caps, and a crown capping tool. There is not much advice one can give on the purchase of such items, they are subconsciously acquired over a period of time such that eventually one ends up with a surplus. In fact, it is quite important to condition yourself NOT to be tempted to buy another one of these, or another one of those, when browsing around your home brew shop.

The 'copper' or brewing boiler

A boiler is an item of equipment that can be considered essential to a keen home brewer, particularly if one is going to produce mashed beers. If you are a novice home brewer and are brewing from malt extract, there is no need, initially, to go to the expense of purchasing a special purpose brewing boiler. A large saucepan of sufficient capacity to boil the malt extract and hops is all that is necessary. However, as you progress through your apprenticeship you will find the purchase of a suitable boiler desirable, and if you mash your beers you will find one essential. Unless you have a large dixie (not made from iron), capable of holding about six gallons of water, the boiler is probably the only expensive item of equipment that can not be improvised by utilising domestic equipment.

There are several brewing boilers available to the home brewer. All of the purpose made ones are manufactured from food grade polypropylene. They are adequate for our purposes but are not ideal. Home brewing entails a considerable amount of moving of vessels from one level to another. A disadvantage of boilers made from polypropylene is that when they are hot they go 'squidgy' and unstable which makes them difficult to move safely, particularly when they are full. A further disadvantage with the polypropylene boilers is that they are not really large enough for our normal 25 litre quantities of finished beer.

Burco manufacture stainless steel boilers which can be easily adapted for home brewing purposes. These stainless steel boilers have the disadvantage that they are more than twice the cost of a polypropylene boiler, but otherwise they are ideal for our purposes. They are manufactured in 26, 35, and 50 litre capacities. Mine is of 26 litre capacity and is adequate, but, in retrospect, the 35 litre version would have been better. A stainless boiler can be used unmodified, but a useful modification is to fit a perforated false bottom just above the tap outlet. This provides a base onto which the hops can settle after the boil, thereby providing a filter bed to remove the trub during the running-off operation. The false bottom can be manufactured from aluminium, copper, or polypropylene sheet with a large number of 4mm holes drilled in it. Alternatively, two sheets of expanded aluminium mesh can be bolted together, out of register. My particular Burco stainless boiler required the fitting of an additional tap, the original one was far too high up the side of the boiler for effective use.

Second boiler (hot liquor tank)

Some grain brewers have a second boiler which serves as a hot liquor tank. This is used for holding the liquor at the appropriate temperature during the mashing and sparging operation. However, this is more of a luxury than a necessity.

Barrels, bottles etc.

When you have brewed your beer you will obviously need some form of container in which to mature, keep, and from which to dispense your beers. It is conventional for home brewers to bottle their beer, however, the cleaning, sterilisation, filling, and capping of forty beer bottles each time that we brew a 25 litre batch of ale is a quite formidable chore. It is far more convenient and practical to barrel our beer. It is far easier to clean, and far easier to fill a 25 litre barrel than it is to clean and fill forty beer bottles. If you are only an occasional drinker, then bottling is probably preferable to barrelling. However, generally speaking, barrels are the preferred vessel. There are a number of barrels available from home brew shops that are quite suitable for our purpose. It is not necessary to buy the expensive pressure kegs, because decent beer should not need to be artificially pressurised. Other sources of suitable barrels are 25 litre wine barrels, which are often available for a nominal charge from local pubs, and are usually identical to the barrels supplied by home brew shops. Polythene cubes or polypins can also be pressed into service if available.

Carbon dioxide injectors

Carbon dioxide injectors are available from home brew shops. However, real beer should not normally need CO_2 injection. If you are a real beer fan, you should only use the injector to displace the air – do not pressurise your beer. Other uses of the injector are to purge barrels free of air before filling them.

Mash tun

Mashing requires that the grist is steeped in water, accurately maintained at 65°C for a period of up to two hours. For this operation we use a special vessel called a mash tun. Enthusiastic home brewers have experimented with various forms of mash tun over the years with varying degrees of success.

There are two basic types of mash tun; the heated variety, and the well-insulated unheated variety. Because we wish to maintain our mash at a fairly high temperature over a period of up to two hours, it is natural to assume that the best way of doing so is to fit a heater and thermostat – **wrong!** Mashing requires quite close control of temperature if repeatability and total control of mash reactions is to be achieved. The accuracies demanded, although not great, are far greater than any domestic situation requires. The thermostatic control of a bulk of grain within a volume of water is a fairly complicated process control problem, and quite difficult to reliably perform. The problems are due to thermostat hysterisis (or backlash to use a mechanical engineers term), and temperature overshoot and undershoot caused by the thermal mass and the thermal inertia of the moist grain. Without going into technicalities, the end result of all this is that most types of uninsulated mash tun, that use a heater and thermostat to maintain the desired temperature, will suffer from large temperature fluctuations or oscillations. If a mash tun needs to be heated, then it should be heated with a low wattage heater, which just supplies enough energy to balance the losses. A device known as a 'simmerstat' is a better controller than a thermostat, but modern electronic controls are probably more appropriate. The best mash tuns rely upon excellent thermal insulation to maintain the desired temperature, not a heater.

Types of mashing system

Boiler and grain bag

The boiler and grain bag method is probably the most commonly used mashing technique. In fact I began to mash using this very method. Grain bags are available from home brew suppliers. One simply places the grain into the bag, which is then placed into the boiler which contains an appropriate quantity of pre-heated water maintained at the appropriate temperature. The method suffers from the thermostatic control problems mentioned above, furthermore the 3KW heater fitted to brewing boilers is far too fierce, exaggerating the control problems and giving the danger that the grain near the element may be burned whilst other parts of the mash may be too cold for efficient extraction. Other disadvantages include the fact that the boiler is tied up for mashing duties when it would be better employed heating the sparge liquor, or waiting to collect the sweet wort in readiness for boiling. Also, the technique prevents us from using the grain as a filter bed to clarify the wort.

Commercial mash tun

There are a number of commercially available mash tuns. These are usually no more than the polypropylene brewing boilers with a smaller (1KW) heater fitted. Fortunately, they use a simmerstat as the controller, and not a thermostat. Some are supplied with a perforated false bottom to eliminate the need for the messy grain bag. These are typically uninsulated and suffer from most of the disadvantages of the previous technique. Nevertheless, they work fairly well.

Floating mash tun

The floating mash tun is a mashing method which was advocated by the late Dave Line. It consists of standing a small brewing bin, which is used as the mash tun, into a large boiler full of water maintained at the appropriate mashing temperature. The water jacket thus created around the mash tun helps to maintain the mash at the appropriate temperature. The system works well provided that one manually corrects errors in temperature when necessary by turning the heater on for short bursts. If the heater is used in conjunction with the thermostat large temperature fluctuations can result. The major disadvantage is that one needs a very large boiler to mash in this manner, the problem is further aggravated by the fact that, ideally, we require a tap on our mash tun to facilitate run-off and sparging, the boiler would need to be large enough to accommodate the projecting tap, as well as the bin.

A simple insulated mash tun

As I mentioned earlier, an insulated mash tun will usually produce superior results to a heated mash tun. The mash tun to be described here is an insulated mash tun that very closely imitates a traditional commercial brewery's mash tun. It is relatively cheap to make, uses easily obtainable parts, and performs well.

The system basically consists of two standard brewing bins, one pushed inside the other. The outer bin is thoroughly lagged externally with plastic coated Rockwool or fibreglass strips, intended for lagging hot water tanks. The lagging is available from a D.I.Y. shop or plumbers merchant. The inner bin has a matrix of holes drilled in its base to serve as the false bottom to retain the grain during the run-off and sparging operation. The two bins should be identical except that the outer bin should have a tap fitted, and the inner bin should not. The inner bin should be equipped with a close fitting lid. In contrast to the advice given above regarding fermenting bins, the type of bin employed for this application should be of the highly tapered, bucket shaped, variety, not the tall narrow type, which will not push down far enough inside each other.

Using a scriber or other suitable instrument, carefully mark out the base of the inner bin on a spider web pattern. Drill the appropriate number of 2mm or 3mm holes at the intersections of the grid, taking care not to drill any holes that are spaced less than about 5mm apart to reduce the possibility of weakening the base of the bin. The hole size is not critical. My bin has a 280mm (11inch) base and has about 400, 3mm (11/64″) holes drilled symmetrically around it. The outer bin is unmodified with the exception of having a tap fitted. The tap should be fitted fairly close to the bottom to reduce the amount of wasted space at the bottom of the bin, but don't fit the tap so low that it prevents the bin being stood on a flat surface!

The tun is assembled by pushing the previously drilled inner bin down into the outer bin as far as it will go, it should rest upon the outer bin tap fixing nut.

Insulating the mash tun

There are two methods of insulating the bin:

The simplest method is simply wrap the strips of plastic covered insulation around the outside of the outer bin, secured in position by ties or by adhesive tape. Tapes can be stitched to the strips of insulation in order to facilitate assembly if desired. During the mash the lid is fitted to the inner bin and more strips of insulation are laid on the top to reduce the heat loss through the lid.

The second insulation method entails making up a wooden box, a little larger than the assembled tun. The inner sides, and lid of the box are lined with the insulating strips. The strips can be fixed to the sides of the box with drawing pins. During the mashing operation the tun is simply stood in the box and the lid closed.

In practice it will be found that, in a cold garage during December, either version will lose less than 2°C over a two hour mash period. A messy grain bag is not used, and the tun can be easily dismantled to facilitate cleaning. Grain disposal is effected by simply pulling the two bins apart, tipping the grains out, and then washing the contraption down with a garden hose.

Heating the mash tun.

If you are using an insulated mash tun and you feel that the heat loss from your mash tun over the two hour mashing period is too great, one way of reducing the loss is to fit a heating belt around the tun, under the insulation. Two 25W brewbelts fitted around the tun, or a 55W fermenting mat under the tun (and insulation) will probably suffice. A 75W or 100W W gardeners soil warming cable wrapped around the outside of the bin, giving a fairly even distribution of heat, is probably best. A careful check should be kept on temperature to ensure that it remains constant, switching off the heater if the temperature begins to rise.

If you wish to experiment with the temperature programmed, or decoction type of mashing system, a much larger heater will be required in order to raise the temperature to the new level after the protein rest period. In a well insulated system, a 500 watt heater will raise the temperature of our mash by 10°C in well under half an hour, which is more than adequate for this application. Kettle elements are suitable heaters for this purposes. A 500 watt element would be ideal, however, 1000 Watts (1KW) is the lowest wattage of kettle element that is easily obtainable. Raising the temperature by means of a heater should be performed gently to obviate the risk of burning the grain or producing local hot-spots which could damage the enzymes.

Some temperature control can be obtained by using a Simmerstat type of controller. These are used in electric cookers and can be purchased from electrical wholesalers. Remember that a Simmerstat is **not** a thermostat and does not control the temperature directly, it merely reduces the amount of energy going into the system. A careful eye must still be kept on the temerature, readjusting the simmerstat if necessary. An electric drill speed controller or a dimmer switch could also be used, providing they are of adequate rating, however, the simmerstat is preferred.

Sparging equipment

When the mash has been completed and the sweet wort run off, it will be necessary to rinse the grains free of any valuable sugars which may be trapped within. This operation is known as sparging and is described in greater detail elsewhere. Sparging should be conducted gently to prevent the filter bed of grain in the bottom of the tun from cracking or blocking. Beginners to mashing often gently pour hot water over the grains using an ordinary jug, this technique does break up the mash bed with the risk of hazy beer. However, it is an easy solution. Eventually some form of spray head is usually fabricated. This is most often the spraying rose from a indoor plant waterer, or from a garden watering can. A spray ring can be fabricated from small bore copper or stainless steel tubing.

Cooling equipment

Rapidly cooling the wort after the boil is one of the biggest problems facing the home brewer. Most brewers simply transfer the hot wort into a brewing bin, stand the bin in a bath of cold water, and wait untill the wort has cooled. This method is quite inefficient, and prone to messy accidents, but much better than nothing.

A simple wort cooler

A suitable compromise is 'Wheelers Wonderful Wort Cooler': This consists of a coil of 15mm flexible copper pipe, fixed to the inside of a brewers bin by means of standard tank flanges. The hot wort is run from the boiler into the bin, and cold water is run through the coil of copper pipe until the wort has cooled to the desired temperature.

Malt Mill

Malt must be crushed or cracked before mashing to enable the water in the mash to reach the starch in the endosperm of the grain. It is usual for the home brewer to buy his grain ready cracked. If one buys his grain uncracked or is experimenting with other types of grain, then some sort of mill will be required. There are various methods of cracking grain that have been devised by home brewers over the years, all of them are by necessity rather slow and laborious. The simplest method is put small quantities of grain onto a large tray, cover the tray with a piece of cloth to prevent the grain shooting all over the place, and then lightly crush the grain by means of running a rolling pin back and forth across the tray. Other methods include using a modified coffee mill, and a very popular method is to use a unmodified meat mincer.

Equipment materials

The materials from which our equipment is made deserves a brief mention here. You can be sure that equipment purchased from your home brew shop is compatible with the home brewing process. But if we press household equipment or vessels into service, some care is warranted.

Most commercial equipment is either made from food grade polythene or food grade polypropylene. Food grade polythene is the cheaper material but it has the disadvantage that it is quite soft and therefore scratches easily, scratches are potential 'bug' traps. Furthermore polythene begins to soften and go 'squidqy' at about 60°C making it unsuitable for very hot liquids, whereas polypropylene is stable up to boiling point. Any plastic utensils, not intended for food or brewing use, should be of the plain uncoloured variety. The theory being that the dyes used may be toxic or will taint the beer.

When mashing or boiling, polypropylene, aluminium, copper, or stainless steel vessels are suitable. Iron vessels are not! Brewers wort is by nature acidic, and it will attack the iron vessel putting iron-ions into your wort. This may not seem a bad thing, particularly if you are over forty and need fortifying, but iron has a detrimental effect on beer. The iron will interfere with the enzymic processes during the brewing process causing numerous problems. It will try to poison your yeast, the reaction will raise the pH of your wort, and the final beer will be hazy.

A quick word about aluminium. Aluminium is attacked by most alkalis, most proprietry cleaners or sterilisers are based upon alkaline materials. Read the instructions on any cleaner to ensure that it is compatible before using it on aluminium.

Work staging

When mashing it is advantageous to have some sort of support for your brewing utensils, arranged on three levels. During the sparging operation the mash tun should be situated above the boiler so that the runnings can flow directly into the boiler, however, the hot liquor tank needs to be above the level of the mash tun such that sparging can be accomplished. I am not suggesting anything should be constructed to facilitate this, but some sort of improvisation should be considered before beginning to mash. The floor, plus a Workmate, plus a garage work-bench; or possibly, the floor, plus a kitchen chair, plus the kitchen work-top. I am sure that you will devise something!

5 Grain, sugar, malt extract

The Barley

The primary ingredient of beer is malted barley. Barley for English brewing is traditionally a specially selected variety of English two-rowed barley. English brewing barley is usually specially grown, because it is important that brewing barley should have a low protein content. An excess of protein and certain other nitrogenous substances will encourage haze to be formed in the finished beer. Fortunately, the English climate, cultivation techniques, and strain of barley assists in the production of a low protein/nitrogen product. English brewing barley is usually grown at a lower density per acre than barley used for other purposes, and the use of nitrogen based fertilisers is avoided.

The barley grain consists, essentially, of two parts: the inner part, called the endosperm which is mostly starch; and the outer part, called the aleurone layer, which is a tough outer wall surrounding the endosperm and consists of a number of complex proteins. The starch contained in the endosperm is important because it is broken down during mashing into maltose (a complex sugar) to yield fermentable sugars, and ultimately beer. The proteins contained in the aleurone layer are just as important because they are high molecular weight nitrogenous substances which are broken down during malting into simpler, soluble, low molecular weight nitrogenous substances, to yield amino acids, peptides, and most importantly, enzymes. The amino acids, peptides, and other forms of assimilable nitrogen are important to the yeast, but an excess of these will provide food for bacteria during storage, the lactic acid bacteria in particular.

A good sample of barley suitable for brewing purposes should have a uniform grain size, a powdery endosperm, it should be of the proper colour, and, of course, the nitrogen level should be correct. Before a maltster buys barley he tests a sample to ensure that it meets his requirements and that it malts satisfactorily.

During the malting process a group of enzymes break down proteins in the outer wall of the barley (the aleurone layer) to render the starch contained in the endosperm open to attack. In the old days, these enzymes were known collectively by the old fashioned name of cytase, but in a more modern vein, the two most important enzymes groups are known as proteases (proteinase), and peptideases (peptidase), and each group consists of a number of individual enzymes. The proteases (enzymes that attack protein), also degrade the small amount of protein which is contained in the endosperm itself, this protein can be considered to be in the spaces between the starch molecules and act as a binder. The degradation of these 'binding' proteins renders the starch open to attack by other enzymes during the subsequent mashing process.

The protein degradation is known as modification, a fully modified malt is one where as much of the protein as possible has been degraded by the malting process and is typical of English malts. A poorly modified malt is one where some of the protein remains undegraded and was typical of lager malts of over a hundred years ago, and requires a decoction mash to complete the conversion. Poorly modified malt was supposedly due to the poorer quality, high nitrogen, barley and poorer malting skills of the Continentals. However, high nitrogen, poorly modified malts are rich in enzymes, and these enzymes can be exploited by the decoction mash process to mash a very high proportion of other cereals. It is true that the Germans were unable to match the clarity and brilliance of English pale ales until they developed the decoction system; but modern lager malts are more fully modified than those of yesteryear.

The maltster uses nitrogen content as a guide to the malting quality of his barley. The protein contained in the aleurone layer is a nitrogenous compound, therefore a barley which has a high nitrogen content will have a higher ratio of protein to starch than will a barley of low nitrogen content. The higher level of protein could give rise to hazes being formed in the beer, whereas the lower level of starch will provide a lower level of fermentable extract, making the malt less efficient. However the important enzymes are also nitrogenous substances, therefore a barley which has a low nitrogen content would also have a low enzymic activity, which again may be undesirable. As you will realise, the nitrogen content of barley, and the nitrogen content of the resultant malt is very important, and must be held within certain limits if the correct balance of protein, starch, and enzymic activity is to be achieved. In general, barleys of differing nitrogen contents are used to make different types of malt. A high nitrogen malt would have a lower fermentable extract, and a higher level of undesirable proteins than would a low nitrogen malt, but it would also have a high level of enzymic activity which is an advantage in some applications. The opposite would be true of a low nitrogen malt. In general, low and medium nitrogen barleys are used to make our true malts, whereas high nitrogen barleys are used to make coloured malts and some adjuncts.

Two other important enzymes are contained in our barley and ultimately in our malt; namely alpha-amylase and beta-amylase. These enzymes are not particularly active during malting, but are utilised during mashing, and serve to break down the starch contained in the endosperm into sugars which will be fermented by the yeast. These two enzymes are known as diastatic enzymes and are described in more detail in Chapter 9, however, this brings us on to the diastatic power of malt. The diastatic power of the malt is a measure of the quantity of the diastatic enzymes present in the malt, and is therefore a measure of the speed at which starch is converted into sugars. In general, most malts have a quantity of diastatic enzymes surplus to requirements, and these enzymes can be effectively used to convert the starch in other cereals into fermentable sugars. These cereals, such as torrified barley, flaked barley, or wheat flour, contain convertible starch, but do not contain the diastatic enzymes necessary to effect that conversion. The higher the diastatic power of the malt, the greater is the quantity of these cereals which can be effectively converted. Highly diastatic malts can have a penalty; the diastatic enzymes are more abundant in high nitrogen malts, and will therefore give a higher risk of haze formation, and a lower fermentable yield.

The kilning stage of malt production dries the malt to well defined levels of moisture content. The basic malts are dried at relatively low temperatures to preserve the diastatic enzymes that we require during our mashing stage, and the proteinase which is necessary for lager production in particular. Lager malt, pale malt, and mild ale malt are typically dried to 3.8, 3, and 2.8 percent moisture content respectively and, of course, their colours are progressively darker. Roasted malts such as chocolate malt or black malt are quickly dried at high temperatures, which destroys the enzymes but colours the malt accordingly.

Pale malt

Pale Malt, as its name implies, is pale in colour. It is the basic ingredient of pale ales and bitters, but finds application in almost any type of English beer. It is a fully modified malt that has been kilned at a low temperature for a long period, until its moisture content is about 3%. Pale malt has good diastatic activity and can be used to assist the conversion of a certain amount of non diastatic cereal.

Mild ale malt

Mild ale malt is initially prepared in the same way as pale malt, except that a higher nitrogen barley is used, it is kilned at a slightly higher temperature and for longer than pale malt to reduce its moisture content to about 2.8% . As one would expect, mild ale malt is darker than pale ale malt, and has a slightly lower extract. Mild ale malt has a higher diastatic activity than pale malt, allowing a higher proportion of adjuncts to be used in the grist makeup. A higher level of adjuncts is typical of mild ale production and provides the characteristic flavours of mild ale.

Amber malt

Amber malt is prepared by rapidly heating fully cured mild ale malt to about 100°C in a kiln, and then slowly allowing the temperature to rise upto a maximum of about 150°C. As soon as the malt has turned the correct colour it is allowed to cool. Amber malt has a characteristic biscuity taste and finds application in mild ales, brown ales, old ales, and some bitters. The high temperatures involved in its production destroys the enzymes, therefore amber malt has little diastatic activity but it does yield fermentable extract if mashed alongside a diastatic malt.

Crystal malt

Crystal malt, sometimes referred to as caramel malt, is prepared by wetting high nitrogen green malt (unkilned), heating to 65°C in a closed vessel and holding this temperature until the starch in the endosperm has been hydrolysed into a sugary syrup. The grains are then kilned at approximately 250°C which dries the malt, caramelizes some of the sugar, and colours the mass to a light reddish tint. When the grain has cooled it forms a solid sugary mass. Crystal malt is a very common ingredient in English style bitters and it imparts a distinctive nutty flavour. Crystal malt contains a high proportion of dextrins and other non fermentable sugars and it will therefore provide a degree of residual sweetness to the finished beer. Crystal malt has had its starch converted to sugars during manufacture and does not need to be mashed during the brewing process. A ten to fifteen minute steep in a saucepan of hot or boiling water is sufficient to extract the desired properties. The malt will need to be strained and rinsed afterwards to ensure complete removal of the husks from the sugars. In grain brewing (as opposed to malt extract brewing), it is usual to put the crystal malt into the mash tun along with the pale malt. This is done because the mash tun happens to be a convenient place to introduce it into the brewing process, and it saves a separate steeping and straining operation. Crystal malt should not comprise more than about 20% of the total weight of grist in bitters or approximately 30% in mild ales.

Chocolate malt

This is made by roasting high nitrogen malt in a kiln at temperatures of up to 230°C until the malt is the desired colour. The malt is then rapidly quenched to prevent further colour change.

Chocolate malt was used extensively in the past to provide colour, flavour and body to the darker beers and old ales. A number of famous commercial beers have a proportion of chocolate malt in their grist make up. It provides a very pleasant characteristic flavour. Chocolate malt should be used in quite small proportions, usually less than 12 grams per litre (2 oz per gallon) otherwise its flavour becomes overriding. At this low level of concentration, the fermentable extract can be ignored for all practical purposes. Malt extract brewers are able to use chocolate malt by crushing and then boiling it in a small quantity of water for ten or fifteen minutes, straining off the water into the fermentation vessel. Grain brewers should put chocolate malt into the mash tun along with the other ingredients, where the small amount of fermentablity will be extracted and the flavour imparted will be much rounder.

Black malt

This is made in the same way as chocolate malt, except that the darkening of the malt is allowed to proceed much further before the grain is quenched. The high temperatures involved destroy the enzymes and some of the starch contained in the malt, therefore dark malts have no diastatic activity, and a lower fermentable extract than other malts. They are used to add flavour and colour to mild beers, porters, and stouts. The flavour imparted by dark malts is similar to roast barley except that black malt is somewhat less dry. Black malt should not be used in quantities in excess of 10% of grist make up, considerably less is usual.

Roast barley

Roast barley is unmalted barley that has been roasted in a kiln until it is burnt. It is again used to alter the colour and flavour of mild ales, porters, and stouts in particular. It has similar properties to the dark malts above, except that the flavour imparted by roast barley, although similar, is much smoother and drier than black malt. It also contributes to head colour and retention. It promotes a similar head to that of Guinness. Again malt extract brewers can use roast barley without mashing. Like the dark malts, roast barley is used at very low concentrations otherwise its flavour becomes overpowering.

Lager malts

Lager malts are traditionally poorly modified malts, meaning that the protein in the endosperm wall is not completely converted into low order nitrogens by the malting process. Lager malts are traditionally mashed using the continental decoction mash, which feature a low temperature protein rest period prior to the mash proper. During this period an enzyme 'proteinase', which is supplied by the malt, completes the conversion of proteins into simpler nitrogenous substances. If we mashed traditional lager malt by the British infusion mashing method, we would run the risk of promoting a protein haze in our beer due to the high level of unmodified protein present in solution.

However, modern lager malts are fully modified and we can safely use them in our infusion mash. The continental decoction mash is ideally suited for high adjunct brewing, because the proteinase supplied by the lager malt can be utilised to convert the proteins in other cereals. It is important that genuine lager malt should be rich in this particular enzyme if a high proportion of unmalted cereals are to be used in the recipe. The reason for the very pale colour of traditional lager malt is due to the fact that a low degree of kilning is essential to prevent destruction of the very temperature sensitive proteinase. **Pilsen** lager malt is very pale in colour, is highly diastatic, and high in proteinase. **Munich** lager malt is very much darker than Pilsen malt and has a lower level of diastatic activity. **Cara pils** malt is the continental equivalent of crystal malt, it is darker than Munich malt and it has no diastatic activity.

Selecting, purchasing, and using malts

All malts and some adjuncts need to be cracked or lightly crushed (milled) before use. Malt needs to be crushed to the correct degree if proper extraction is to be achieved, without impairing mash tun run off. Fortunately, all home brew shops sell malt ready crushed, thereby saving us the difficulty of doing it ourself. Malt, in its crushed form, is hygroscopic and if not properly stored will absorb moisture from the atmosphere and quickly go **slack**. Ensure that the malt is in good condition if purchased ready milled, ensure that the grains are plump and that the endosperm is crisp but not hard, flinty or powdery. You should store ready crushed malt in a cool dry place.

Malt extract

Malt extracts are the mainstay of the home brewing hobby. The majority of home brewers use malt extract as their basic source of fermentable sugars, and all ordinary beer kits are based upon malt extract. Malt extract brewing is quick and simple, and there is no doubt that the home brewing industry would not have grown to its current size had it not been for the availability of this product. Malt extract can be manufactured in a number of ways; with some of these methods the resulting syrup should not be called malt extract, but more properly barley syrups or corn syrups. Malt extracts are often produced by mashing malted barley in the conventional way, and then concentrating the resultant wort by passing it through a multistage low temperature vacuum evaporator until it is concentrated to about 80% solids. An important omission from the malt extract manufacturing process is the wort boil, and probably accounts for the off-flavours and clarity problems often associated with extract and beer kit brewing.

Another way of producing a similar extract uses a mash of raw barley plus the addition of industrial enzymes, this should more properly called barley syrup. A very similar product can be manufactured from corn plus industrial enzymes. There are a whole range of malt extracts available; hopped, unhopped, mild flavoured, strong flavoured, light, medium or dark coloured, diastatic and non diastatic.

Malt extracts have a number of uses to the grain brewer; making yeast starters, as an additional source of fermentable extract, or as source of diastatic enzymes.

MALT ADJUNCTS

For our purposes the term malt adjuncts refers to grain, malted or unmalted, that is capable of producing fermentable extract in our wort but does not possess the enzymes necessary to effect the conversion of starch into fermentable sugars. Adjuncts draw upon enzymes supplied by the pale malt in the mash. All adjuncts must be mashed, alongside malted barley or some other source of enzymes such as diastatic malt extract in order to effect conversion. Strictly speaking, sugars, syrups, crystal malt, black malts, or roast barley, are not considered to be adjuncts because they do not need conversion by the enzymes contained in the pale malt.

The term 'adjuncts', although technically correct, is much misunderstood. For some inexplicable reason many people have acquired the notion that all brewing adjuncts are inferior ingredients which are included in recipes purely for reasons of economy and therefore must be undesirable. I am sure that this is due to a basic misunderstanding of the term 'adjunct'. It is true that some adjuncts will effect a small gain in economy but it is not really significant. Adjuncts are not used in very large quantities. Furthermore, these materials are manufactured and processed, and like malted barley, are not exactly given to the brewers free of charge.

In general, adjuncts are used to provide subtle changes in flavour or to improve the brewing process in one way or another. Apart from modifying the flavour of beers, brewing adjuncts can assist the brewer in many ways, such as aiding mash tun run-off, assisting clearing, improving head retention, improving beer stability, and reducing protein haze.

Malt adjuncts must be used intelligently, in fact if they are used in too high proportion they will often have the opposite effect to that desired and will degrade the beer. As a rule the combined weight of adjuncts should not exceed about 20% of the total weight of the grist. If adjuncts are used in too high a proportion problems soon begin to manifest themselves. Mash tun run-off may be impaired due incorrect grist particle size, or due to too high a proportion of beta-glucan gums being extracted from unmalted grains. Mash tun conversion problems may occur due to a deficiency of the necessary enzymes, hazes may result due to a high proportion of undegraded protein being present, and yeast activity may be impaired due to a low level of assimilable nitrogen in the wort.

Remember that all adjuncts must be mashed and rely upon enzymes supplied by the pale malt to effect the conversion of the starch into sugar. It is also important to remember that unmalted grains have not had their protein degraded, therefore, unless the manufacturing process degrades the protein, or unless you are mashing by the decoction method, this protein will still be present in the adjunct, and will give the risk of a protein haze being formed in the beer.

Torrefied grains, flakes, grits.

One of the reasons for malting our barley is to render the starches in the endosperm into a form suitable for attack by the enzymes. However, there are methods other than malting which will render the starches in cereals open to attack. A common method is some form of heat treatment. The heat treatment gelatinises the starch which renders it open to attack by the enzymes contained in our pale malt.

Torrified grains are grains that have been 'popped' in a similar manner to popped corn. The high temperature involved in popping explodes the endosperm of the grain and gelatinises the starch rendering it open to attack. Torrified grains can be used in our mash tun directly without any form of pre-treatment.

Flakes are made by steaming the grain until it swells and then rolling it through heated rollers. The high temperatures destroy the aleurone layer, and gelatinises the starch, rendering it open to attack. Flakes can also be used in our mash tun directly without any form of pre-treatment.

Grits are unmalted grains that have been milled to provide a smaller particle size, thereby exposing a greater surface area. They usually cannot be used in our mash tun directly. We have to cook them first to gelatinise the starch. The only exception to this rule is wheat. The gelatinisation temperature of wheat happens to coincide with our mash temperature, enabling us to use it directly. The gelatinisation temperature of most other grains is much higher than our mash temperature. With the exception of wheat flour, grits do not find much favour in English brewing practice. Continental and American breweries that use a high proportion of adjuncts usually have a separate cereal cooker adjacent to the mash tun which is used to perform this gelatinisation process.

Grits are best suited to the continental decoction method of mashing, particularly if used in large quantities. They are unmalted grains that are merely ground to a small particle size. The protein rich aleurone layer has not been broken down into simpler substances by the milling process. It is still present in the flour, and can therefore give rise to protein haze problems.

Wheat flour

Brewers wheat flour is probably the most commonly used adjunct in Britain. There is hardly a brewery in the country that does not use a proportion of wheat flour in its grist make up. In small quantities the effect of wheat on flavour is hardly noticeable, it merely rounds it off slightly by counteracting harshness. In larger quantities the wheaty flavour becomes apparent, which is quite pleasant. However, wheat flour's main benefit may not be apparent to the drinker. Its inclusion by the brewer improves head retention, and being low in nitrogen produces a beer with less haze potential. Typical proportions are between 5 and

10% of the total weight of the grist. It has a similar extract to pale malt and in moderation can be substituted directly for it. The only disadvantage with wheat flour, particularly if used in too high a proportion, is that it can hinder mash tun run-off by blocking the filter bed of spent grains. It should be stressed that domestic flour is not really suitable for brewing. Brewers wheat flour is specially ground to a very small particle size, then the flour is graded such that the particle size is within strict limits. Wheat flour does not need to be cooked because it's gelatinisation temperature is the same as our mashing temperature. It can be put directly into the mash tun.

Malted wheat

Malted wheat has only recently gained in popularity in home brewing circles. It provides a rather unique wheat flavour to beers, much more pronounced than unmalted wheat flour. It is available as both grain or flakes. It is lovely stuff, so beware! You will probably eat more of it than you use for brewing. Malted wheat is used in relatively small proportions of the grist, usually at a rate of less than 6 grams per litre (1 oz. per gallon).

Raw barley

Raw barley has been used as an adjunct in the past, and was used by a number of breweries during the second world war to try to combat malt shortages. Barley can be used at up to fifteen percent of the grist before serious problems begin to show themselves. Barley needs to be carefully milled such that the husk remains intact to provide adequate mash tun drainage, whilst the endosperm is adequately crushed to ensure efficient extraction. Barley brewing is best suited to the decoction mash, although it can be used carefully in the infusion mash. Interest in raw barley brewing has recently been revived due the low cost of barley compared to malt. By using the decoction mash and adding enzymes to the mash it is possible, although not recommended, to use up to eighty percent raw barley in the grist.

Flaked barley

Flaked barley is another adjunct that is commonly used in both commercial and home brewing. It can be used in our mash tun directly. It imparts a grainy flavour to beers and it assists in head formation and retention. Like most unmalted grains, its use increases the risk of haze formation. It is quite a common ingredient in bitters, but it is used in higher proportions in dark milds and stouts where its rich grainy flavour is much appreciated.

Torrified barley

Torrified barley is grain that has been popped in a similar manner to pop-corn. This adjunct has not found a wide acceptance in home brewing circles, probably because the flavour that it imparts is similar to that of flaked barley, although somewhat drier. Its inclusion in bitters and milds adds body and flavour and is therefore quite a valuable adjunct. Commercial brewers like to use a small amount of torrified barley because it considerably aids mash tun run-off, preventing the goods setting firm. You can produce your own torrified barley from raw barley grains by heating them in a saucepan until they pop, in exactly the same way as you would make pop corn. Do not do as I did, and forget to put a lid on the saucepan, otherwise you will have popped barley flying all over the kitchen. Again torrified barley does not need to be cooked.

Flaked maize

Maize (corn) is one of the earliest of malt adjuncts, and world wide, probably one of the most widely used. Flaked maize imparts a characteristic corny flavour to beers and is useful, in moderate quantities, to give character and distinction to delicately flavoured beers. It is almost nitrogen free and is therefore useful as a nitrogen dilutent. It is a very predominate adjunct in Australian and American beers and is used by them in fairly high proportions, presumably because it is a cheap method of diluting the high nitrogen content of their malt, which would otherwise cause a protein haze. It does not enjoy the same sort of popularity in England. British brewing practice favours the use of commercially produced glucose syrups, many of these are produced from maize. It is possible for the British brewer to impart similar qualities to his beers by the use of these syrups, with or without the 'corny' flavour of flaked maize, which generally does not find favour with the English palate. Flaked maize is made by steaming corn until it swells and then rolling it through heated rollers. Breakfast type corn flakes are nothing other than flaked maize.

Maize grits

Maize grits also find favour with American and Australian breweries. It imparts similar characteristics to the flakes above. Domestic corn flour is a maize grit, although not of brewing quality, it can be used with care. Maize grit needs to be cooked before use for fifteen minutes at 70°C to gelatinise the starch. If small quantities are used it can be infusion mashed after cooking, but if large proportions are used it should be decoction mashed as in the continental method of brewing.

Flaked rice and rice grits

The use of flaked rice and rice grits was pioneered by the Australian and American breweries and is not much used in this country. It is almost tasteless and colourless and is again a nitrogen dilutent. Its main advantage is that it is also a colour dilutent and is useful in producing the thin, very lightly coloured beers that are typical of American brewing practice. Rice should not be used for the production of traditional English beer. It has absolutely nothing going for it. Flaked rice can be used directly in our mash tun, but grits will need cooking in a small volume of water for fifteen minutes at 70°C before adding to the mash tun (complete with water). Domestic rice can be used by first breaking the grain as much as is practical with a rolling pin and then cooking as above. Rice is best suited to the decoction mashing method.

Malted oats

Brewers located in hard water areas often used a proportion of crushed malted oats in their grist make-up (4% to 8%) when brewing stouts or porter. It is said that the mellow flavour extracted from the oats counteracted the harshness imposed by the hard water.

Oatmeal, Rolled Oats

Unmalted oatmeal was originally included in many brewers' grist makeup as an economy measure during the war. Oatmeal throws a haze, so its inclusion in any quantity was limited to dark beers and stouts, which at that time were the most popular beers anyway. Oatmeal stouts became very popular, probably due to their supposedly nutritive benefit. They have only recently disappeared as a result of consumer protection acts. When the country got back onto an economic footing after the war, no self respecting brewer would continue to throw significant quantities of oatmeal in his grist, although many breweries continued to market a fluid they called oatmeal stout!

SUGARS

There are many different classes of sugar which can be derived from a variety of materials. Some sugars are fermentable by brewers yeast, but there are a number of sugars that the yeast is unable to ferment or can only ferment very slowly. In general, sugars derived from cane (or beet) are totally fermentable, whereas specialised brewing sugars that are derived from barley or corn contain a proportion of sugars that are non fermentable, thereby imparting residual sweetness and body to our beer.

Sugar can alter the flavour and quality of our beer to a certain degree, but an excess of cane sugar will produce a particularly thin characterless beer. The best quality beers incorporate no sugar at all; although moderate amounts of sugar can be incorporated into beer recipes without any detrimental effect. Sugar can be usefully employed to modify the characteristics of your beer, particularly if a fairly high strength dryish beer is desired. Sugar is a nitrogen dilutent which makes it useful for reducing the risk of a protein haze forming in beer. The major reason that home brew has a bad reputation for providing its imbibers with a nasty hangover is not its strength, as is commonly believed, but the fact that a much too high proportion of cane sugar has been employed in its make up. Take it from me that a high quality all malt brew if drunk to a moderate excess will not give you a hangover the following morning. Having said that, it is also true that many home brewers make their beers far too strong for sensible social drinking. Cane sugar is almost totally fermentable, and the addition of cane sugar has the effect of drying and thinning a beer. You can not sweeten a beer by adding cane sugar. Sugar is described in more detail in the chapter; 'Yeast and fermentation'.

White sugar

White household sugar is the form of sugar most commonly used by home brewers, although it is not used in commercial brewing practice. Cane sugar (sucrose), is a mixture of glucose and fructose. During fermentation brewers yeast releases an enzyme called **invertase** which breaks down the sugar into its component parts, ie, glucose, and fructose. The use of white sugar will have the effect of thinning your beer and giving it a dry flavour, white cane sugar is 100% fermentable, leaving no residual sweetness. If you want a sweeter beer, use more malt, less sugar. Beet sugar is usually avoided by commercial breweries, it is said to encourage poor fermentation and ropiness (a bacterial infection), although I doubt very much if this is true with modern refining processes.

Brown sugars

Brown sugars are very commonly used in home brewing practice. They are the partially refined, unbleached brothers of white sugar. As a consequence of being partially refined they are darker in colour and contain more solids than their white counterparts. When used in brewing they impart colour, and a smooth round flavour which is particularly valuable in milds, stouts, and brown ales. Take care when purchasing brown sugar to ensure that it is the real thing. It has been the practice of refiners in the past to dye white sugar – brown! This may be fine for coffee but is pretty useless from our point of view. I have not encountered the imitation stuff myself, but there was a bit of a 'hoo-haa' about it in the national press quite recently. Brown sugar is available in several varieties, brown, soft brown, demerara, Barbados, etc., all impart slightly different flavours to the beer.

Invert sugar

This is the stuff that breweries use. Invert sugar is partially refined cane sugar that has been already inverted into its component parts (ie, glucose, fructose, and residual non fermentable sugars) by acid treatment. This saves the yeast and its friendly enzyme **invertase** from the bother of doing the job itself and therefore speeds up fermentation. Brewers also feel that it does not produce a harsh tang, or produce a hang-over as does its non inverted or domestic counterparts.

There are various grades of invert sugar which are simply known as No.1, No.2, and No.3. They differ mostly in terms of the colour and flavour imparted, No.3 being the darkest. They are available from some home brew suppliers. If in difficulty, Tate and Lyles Golden Syrup is a readily obtainable form of invert sugar, or alternatively you can make your own:

You can invert domestic cane sugar by dissolving two pounds of brown or white sugar per pint of water in a saucepan, adding a teaspoon of citric acid and simmering for a few minutes. The acid in solution can then be neutralised again by adding a teaspoon of sodium bicarbonate during cooling. Neutrality of the solution can be tested, when cool, with pH indicator papers. Do not do as some writers suggest and add the acid to the sugar and boil it along with the wort in the copper. Some very complex chemical reactions take place during the wort boiling phase of our beer production, and messing around with the acidity (Ph) in this way is quite likely to have a detrimental effect on the final quality.

Invert sugar has an extra molecule of water in its makeup, and is therefore heavier than its non inverted counterpart. If you are buying commercial invert sugar, you will need to use about twenty percent more (by weight) than if you were using non inverted sugar.

Glucose (pure)

Pure glucose either as chips or in syrup form is another sugar that is available to both breweries and amateurs alike. Glucose is completely fermentable and leaves no residual sweetness. It has the effect of promoting a particularly dry beer. Despite popular belief, pure glucose is not often used in commercial brewing practice, it has become confused with the more general (and incorrect) term of glucose syrup and glucose chips to be described below. Pure glucose syrup is expensive to produce, and for brewing purposes at least, it has very little in the way of advantages over the use of invert cane sugar and its derivatives. Cane sugar is a mixture of glucose and fructose, both of which are completely fermentable by the yeast. The glucose syrups available in the home brew shops are not pure glucose (or are very unlikely to be).

Glucose syrups (Corn Syrups)

The term glucose syrup is a very general term used incorrectly to describe a whole variety of liquid sugars used by commercial breweries. Glucose syrups are usually produced from maize (corn) by means of industrial enzymes, and are usually not simple sugars, ie, pure glucose. They should more correctly be termed corn or maize syrups. There are a whole range of glucose syrups available, all of which contain differing proportions of glucose, maltose, and dextrose. Those with a high dextrose content will impart some residual sweetness to the beer. All corn syrups contain a proportion of non fermentable sugars (dextrins); therefore the use of a corn syrup does not necessarily dry and thin the flavour of the beer as does cane sugar or pure glucose. It is for this reason that breweries prefer to use corn derived syrups rather than cane sugar. It is more usual for breweries to use a maltose rich corn syrup, rather than a glucose rich syrup and allow the yeast enzymes to convert the maltose into glucose at its own rate. This apparently pleases the yeast, and reduces the possibility of a stuck fermentation, a condition very familiar to wine makers and high gravity brewers who have included too much sugar in their recipe.

Lactose

Lactose is a form of sugar which is not fermentable by brewers yeast. It can therefore, be used to sweeten beers. Lactose can be purchased from your home brew supplier or a chemist. Lactose is derived from milk and is often used to sweeten stouts, hence the old fashioned term 'Milk Stout', now illegal under food labelling acts, and is the reason for the picture of a milk churn on the Mackeson label.

Priming sugars

Commercial breweries have a large number of priming sugars available to them. These sugars vary greatly with respect to the flavour they impart to the finished beer, and to their degree of fermentability. A priming sugar which has a high level of non fermentable sugars in its composition can be used to sweeten a beer after fermentation, whereas a sugar with high level of fermentable sugars will simply provide secondary fermentation and condition in the barrel. It is unlikely that commercial priming sugars will become available to the home brewing fraternity in the near future, but we are in the fortunate position of being able to make our own fairly simply. By using various combinations of cane sugar, glucose syrup, malt extract, wort, or the new artificial sweeteners that are available, we can produce a priming sugar with any degree of fermentability we desire. Making your own priming sugars is covered in the chapter on finishing.

Caramel

Caramel is a substance derived from burnt sugar and is used in beer solely for colouring. Caramel should really have no place in the home brewer's armoury, we should not find it necessary to colour our beer.

The author of probably the worst book on home brewing that I have read, offers the opinion that a good stout can be made from an ordinary beer plus the addition of caramel. The recipe he provides for a 'good enough' stout is a very basic mild ale recipe into which is thrown a very generous helping of gravy browning! If the man likes his beer in this way it is fine by me, but it certainly 'aint' a stout, and it never will be. It is nothing other than a coloured mild ale. Many of us are home brewers because we expect considerably more than good enough.

It is true that some breweries' milds, browns, and stouts are nothing other than light ales and bitters with caramel added, sometimes additionally sweetened with lactose or priming sugars. We tend to follow commercial brewery practice in the home brewing field, but commercial brewery practice is by no means always good practice. It is interesting to note that the sales of these mediocre products, and the fortunes of the breweries concerned, have rapidly declined, whereas the sales of quality products have continued to thrive.

Guinness and Mackeson are very different beers, both are called stouts, both can be found in nearly every pub in the country irrespective of brewer, both are famous all over the world and are available in over 60 different countries. Why do you think that this should be? I suspect that it is because they are NOT mediocre mild ales with a dollop of gravy browning added!

6 The hops

You are probably quite aware of the fact that beer is made from malted barley, and that hops supply bitterness, aroma, and preservative properties to our beer. But if you ask a number of laymen, 'What is beer made from?', you will probably be astounded to learn of the number of people that give the simple reply, 'Hops', with no mention of malt or barley. A large number of people are quite unaware of the fact that the primary ingredient of beer (apart from water) is malted barley. This is a hangover from the days, not so long ago, when thousands of people, known as mummers, would go hop picking for their annual holiday. When these people asked what the hops were used for, they were given the truthful reply 'Making beer'. It would be logical for them to assume that hops were the primary ingredient of beer. One major brewery uses this lack of knowledge quite effectively in its advertisements: **'There are more hops in B– T–'** was a well known slogan of a few years ago, but in more modern times this has given way to **'You can taste the hops in B– T–'** which is probably a bit more truthful. This not only gives the impression that drinkers are getting value for money, but it also serves to reinforce the view that beer is made only from hops. I doubt very much if the advertisement would be particularly powerful if they used the quality or quantity of barley as the medium, most people would wonder what on earth barley had to do with beer! It is a strange fact that every year, millions of people slush millions of gallons of beer down their throats, without really knowing how it is made. As I begin to write this chapter on hops, a major brewery has just begun to run a new advertisement on the television, it goes: **'Only the best best hops make the best best bitter'**, which of course is perfectly, perfectly true! (still no mention of the barley though!).

Humulus lupulus

The hop plant Humulus lupulus is a hardy perenial climbing plant which is cultivated for beer making in parts of Kent, Hampshire, Worcestershire and Herefordshire. It can grow to as high as thirty feet, but the growth of cultivated hops is deliberately restricted to heights of between fifteen and eighteen feet depending upon variety, the heights at which they provide the best yield. In the old days of manual hop picking the heights were restricted to about ten feet. After the harvest at the end of each season the plants are cut down to their roots, and the rootstock is left in the ground to overwinter. New shoots begin to appear on the rootstock during April and the strongest looking bines are selected for growth, the weaker ones being pruned away. The plants are trained to grow up strings that are supported from an overhead system of wires. There are usually three or four strings per plant, and usually two bines are allowed to grow up each string. The plants grow very rapidly indeed; from the end of April until about mid June the hop grows from rootstock to the top of the support wires, about eighteen feet.

The hop is dioecious, meaning that the male and female flowers are formed on different plants. Only the female plant is used in the making of English beer. The plant can be fertilised or unfertilised although fertilised plants are the norm in England. Obviously, only the fertilised plants produce seeds, but it matters not for the purpose of brewing whether the hop contains seeds or not. However, seeded plants are richer in lupulins (beta acids) and certain oils and are considered by English brewers to be superior in terms of flavour and aroma to their unseeded counterparts. Continental brewing practice favours unseeded hops. Seeded hops usually have a lower yield of humulins (apha acid) per acre than unseeded hops. To ensure that the plant is fertilised by a known strain which is not going to affect the quality of the hop, the hop farmer places a number of male plants on the windward side of his hop garden.

The very rapid growth of the hop plant makes very heavy demands on the soil and the soil is enriched with a fertiliser which provides potassium, nitrogen, calcium and phosphates in the ratios of about 10:10:5:1. In the past, manure and wood ash were traditionaly used as fertilisers.

Around the beginning of September the hops are ready for picking. The hops must be picked as soon as they are ready, just before they fully ripen. In the past it was common for vast armies of Londoners and Brummies to descend upon the hop growing areas of Kent and Worcestershire respectively to pick the hops. In these more modern times the hops are picked by machines, and thousands of people are deprived of their traditional paid annual holiday.

After picking, the hops need to be dried to a moisture content of about fifteen percent. This was traditionally done in the round oast houses that are a familiar sight around the lanes of Kent. The hops were dried by warm air passing up through the perforated drying room floor, the air being heated by a coal fire situated under the floor. The hops were dried by maintaining them at a temperature of 60°C for a period of about ten hours, a steady draught was maintained through the hops by means of a rotating, right angled chimney, which always faced away from the prevailing wind, creating a suction. The flow rate could be controlled by opening or closing ventilators situated in the base of the oast house. Traditionally the hops are sulphured by burning rock sulphur in the coal fire, this was done to ensure that the hops remain stable and pest free during storage.

On the domestic front, male hops can often be seen in large ornamental gardens, grown for decorative reasons over archways and porches. Their fast growth make them particularly useful in quickly establishing a new garden and they make an excellent summer windbreak if trained along wires or fences. (Food for thought!)

Diseases of the hop

The hop farmer is only a hop farmer, he does not have the advantages of crop rotation available to other farmers. He can suffer from a number endemic soil borne diseases which have built up over centuries of intensive hop farming. These diseases are almost impossible to eradicate completely once they become established. This is entirely due to the very nature of hop farming, and a familiar problem to any farmer who rears the same crop year after year in the same fields.

Verticillum Wilt

Verticillum albo-stratum is the most serious of hop diseases because there is no effective cure, except for complete destruction of the affected plants by burning, and to sterilise the soil in which the plants were growing. V. Wilt also affects cucumbers, chrysanthemums, strawberries, and tomatoes, to name but a few domestic crops, where as far as tomatoes are concerned, it is more commonly known as sleepy disease. V. wilt is a fungus which winters in the soil, enters the roots of the plant and travels up its vascular system to the leaves. The leaves develop yellow spots or a yellow stripe and fall off, thereby returning the disease back to the ground to begin its evil work again next year. It is, in fact, illegal to try to maintain a plant that is suffering from the disease. It should properly be burned.

Downy mildew

Downy mildew was brought into Europe from America and first became noticed around 1878. It is another serious disease for the hop grower because the fungus grows deeply into the plant tissues thus seriously damaging them. It only sends thin threads to the surface of leaves to throw spores. Technically it is not a mildew, because mildews are superficial surface infections which do not grow deep into the tissues of the plant as does this infection. The disease is a particular problem in cold damp weather. It shows itself on the surface as a greyish patch of furry growth on the top of the leaves, coupled with a white deposit on the underside. The disease causes the leaves to wither and die, and the hop cones to deform. A late infection may simply cause dark patches to appear on the cones. The disease can be checked by the application of fungicides but by the time it is detected it is too late to save the plant. Among the domestic crops which are susceptible to downy mildew are onions, peas, cucumber, and lettuce. Most fungi find certain metals such as copper, selenium, and zinc highly toxic. Mildews can be controlled by the application of copper or zinc based fungicides, Bordeaux mixture, or commercial organic fungicides.

Powdery mildew

Powdery mildew is again reputed to have been imported from America and its presence was first noticed at Kew gardens in 1850. Powdery mildew is a true mildew which, unlike downy mildew, is a superficial fungal growth which grows on the surface of leaves forming a grey powdery coating. The mildew requires hot dry conditions for its propagation and usually first appears in June or July. In its initial stages, powdery mildew does not damage the tissues of the plant, therefore the disease can be effectively controlled if it is acted upon as soon as it is detected. Apples, grapes, gooseberries, strawberries, and roses are among the domestic plants that can be affected by powdery mildew. Again the mildew can be controlled by metal based fungicides or commercial fungicides. One of the oldest and most effective measures against mildew is sulphur, and an old remedy for mildew was to paint a mixture of flowers of sulphur and soft soap onto the plants, during the warm weather the sulphur would slowly vapourise and kill the mildew as soon as it started. Powdery mildew can also affect hops in storage. Probably the original reason for sulphuring the hops, by burning rock sulphur in the kiln during drying, was to ensure that mildews and other pests were prevented from damaging the stock.

Hop constituents

During the boil in the copper a complex series of reactions take place between the hops and the constituents of the wort. These reactions are not fully understood, but they contribute to the flavour and aroma of the beer to a large degree, assist in the precipitation of trub, and provide some nutrients for the yeast. The most important constituents that are extracted from the hops during the boil are classified as alpha-acids (humulones), beta-acids (lupulones), and essential oils. The alpha-acids constitute the bittering power of the hop, the beta-acids have important side effects during the boil, and the essential oils constitute the flavour and aroma giving properties of the hop. During the boil, the insoluble alpha-acids and beta-acids contained in the hops react with other constituents of the wort and are isomerised, that is, they are changed into a form that is readily soluble in water. Some of the essential oils distill off during the boil and are lost, some other important hop constituents precipitate out of solution with the trub. This gives rise to the practice of sometimes adding hops to the wort in two or more stages, and of sometimes adding hops to the beer after fermentation. Different properties of the hop are important at these different stages. This leads to hops being broadly classified into three basic categories; alpha hops, aroma hops, and general purpose hops. The brewer has three categories for hops used at different stages of the brewing process namely; Copper Hops, Late Hops, and Dry Hops.

Copper Hops are the hops that are put into the copper at the beginning of the boil, and the primary requirement for the hops used at this stage is that they be high in alpha-acid content and be economical to use. High **Alpha** hops are the most economical form of Copper Hop.

Late Hops are hops that are put into the copper during the last fifteen minutes of the boil to restore some of the flavour and aroma giving properties that are distilled off during the main part of the boil. The hops used at this stage should be of a type and quality commensurate with the type of beer being brewed. If dry hopping is not employed they should be of the very best quality **aroma** hops. The Beta-acid and essential oil content are considered to be of prime importance at this stage. General purpose hops are often employed as late hops.

Dry hopping is the term given to hops that are used after fermentation, sometimes added to the copper just before emptying, but usually added directly to the barrels after filling. The hops used at this stage should be specially selected to impart a first class aroma to the finished beer, and should be the very best quality, **aroma** hops, usually Goldings or Fuggles. The only important characteristic of hops used for dry hopping is the aroma imparted, which is contributed by the essential oil content. High alpha copper hops should not, in general, be used for dry hopping, because they impart a harsh bite to the ale, which becomes more unpleasant as the ale ages. It should be clear that dry hopping only improves the 'hoppy' flavour and aroma, it does not (and can not) increase the bitterness of the finished beer.

Types of hop

There are a very large number of varieties of hop that have been available in the past, however, the last ten years or so have seen a large increase in the number of specially developed varieties available to the grower, recently these new varieties have become much more prominent, and to a large extent have displaced many of the more traditional varieties of hop. These new varieties have been developed to provide higher yields, different proportions of alpha-acids and essential oils, resistance to the most troublesome hop diseases, and suitability to mechanised harvesting. Wye College in Kent is responsible for the development of many of these new varieties, and Wye developed hops now dominate the hop gardens of the world to a very great extent.

Golding

The Golding is one of our traditional varieties of hop, and has been around for about one hundred and fifty years. The Golding has a very fine flavour and aroma and is considered to be the premier hop as regards these characteristics. The Golding is highly susceptible to wilt, but it is grown successfully in the wilt free areas of East Kent, Herefordshire, and Worcestershire. Goldings are not often used alone as copper hops due to their high price and low alpha-acid content, but are more often blended with other hops or used as late hops. The Golding is considered to be the best hop for dry hopping pale ales and bitters, for which it finds its major application. A variety known as Whitbread Goldings Variety is often supplied in home brew shops as Goldings, although not identical, they are very similar to traditional Goldings in flavour and aroma. Styrian Goldings are not Goldings, they are in fact a Fuggle variety grown in Yugoslavia.

Fuggle

Introduced by the infamous Mr. Richard Fuggle of Brenchly in 1875. The Fuggle was at one time Britain's most popular hop. It was used extensively in the darker beers. It is often used as a late hop in pale ales or bitters. Again the Fuggle is susceptible to wilt and has a fairly low yield per acre. With the decline of the darker beers, the Fuggle's importance is now giving way to the more modern wilt resistant varieties of hop. The Fuggle is highly prized for its aroma, and is still used to a large extent as a dry hop in traditional English ales, milds, and bitters.

Bullion

The Bullion is one of the earliest of the Goldings varieties, however, it is not classed as a Golding because its flavour and aroma are very unlike a typical Golding hop. The Bullion produces its own distinctive, fairly powerful flavour. It is a heavy cropper, high in alpha-acid content, and was once much prized as an economical copper hop. In more recent times its popularity has been displaced by the more modern wilt resistant varieties of high alpha-acid hop, such as Target. Bullion accounts for only 2.5% of the hops produced, and its popularity is declining yearly. Bullion is regarded as a general purpose hop.

Northern brewer

Northern Brewer is yet another of the early varieties of hybrid hop. As its name suggests, it figured very prominently in the recipes of a particular Northern Brewers' beers. Like many other traditional hops, the Northern Brewer is being displaced by more modern varieties of hop, in this case Northdown which is similar to Northern Brewer.

Target (Wye)

Target is the result of a breeding programme by Wye College in Kent to produce a variety of hop that is resistant to both wilt and powdery mildew. Target has a high alpha-acid content, is resistant to verticillum wilt, and immune to the most common races of powdery mildew. Target has become Britain's most important hop, accounting for about one third of Britain's total hop production. It has a very high alpha-acid content and therefore finds application mostly as a copper hop. Although it is grown seeded, target has a very low seed content.

Northdown (Wye)

Northdown is another of Wye College's children, a Northern Brewer derivative, which it has largely replaced. It has good flavour and aroma and is, therefore, a general purpose hop, suitable as a copper hop, late hop, or dry hop.

Challenger (Wye)

Challenger is another Wye college hop which has rapidly gained popularity in recent years. Challenger is high in essential oils and is considered to be a general purpose hop. It has a fine aroma and can be usefully employed for copper hopping, late hopping, or dry hopping.

Yeoman (Wye)

Yeoman was introduced by Wye College in 1980. It is very similar to Target in both composition and disease resistance, but its aroma is more mellow making it suitable for lager beers as well as traditional ales. Yeoman is considered to be a copper hop.

Zenith (Wye)

The most recent of Wye College's children, Zenith is high in essential oils, particularly when grown seedless. The aroma imparted is very good.

A bitter bout your alphas

The primary standard by which hops are judged is the alpha acid content. The alpha acid content of a hop is a measure of its bittering power; the beta acid and the essential oil content of a hop constitute its aroma and flavour giving properties. Unfortunately these three components do not complement each other. High alpha hops are often used in the copper to provide economical bittering power, but high alpha hops do not have a pleasing aroma. It is therefore recommended that if high alpha hops are used as the primary bittering power, good quality Goldings or other aroma type hop should be used as late hops or dry hops.

Different varieties of hop impart different degrees of bitterness and different hop flavours and aromas. Some varieties of hop are twice as bitter as other varieties, and the flavour and aroma of some varieties of hop are attractive whereas with other varieties of hop it is objectionable. To confuse matters even further, the bitterness of a particular hop will vary from crop to crop, and from harvest to harvest.

Immediately after the harvest, the alpha-acid content of every batch of hops is measured and this information is supplied to the commercial purchaser as the basis on which to determine the quality of the hops, comparative hopping rates, and ultimately the market price. Obviously if a batch of hops has 20% lower alpha-acid content than the previous batch, the brewer will need to use more hops (25% more) to achieve the same bitterness in his beer and will obviously not be prepared to pay as high a price for them. The other constituents, beta-acids and essential oils, are considered to be present in the same ratios, therefore in this particular case they would also be 20% down on the norm.

Hop storage

Hops are not very stable during storage, and must be stored carefully if the quality of the hop is to be maintained. Hops can oxidize very quickly during storage, and they are also photosensitive. Hops are traditionally packed by mechanically compressing them into the traditional long hop pockets. This high degree of compression helps to exclude air from the bulk of the hops and so retard the oxidization. Furthermore hops are always stored in a cool environment (and in the dark), which also retards the oxidization process. The photosensitivity of hops is also an important factor. Hops are harvested, and are at their best, just before they fully ripen. Exposing hops to sunlight, or any source of light at the correct wavelength, will cause the ripening process to continue and degrade the hop. The breweries of old took great pains to ensure that the hops were never exposed to direct sunlight even while they were waiting to go into the copper. The copper rooms of large breweries were often equipped with large canopies, under which the hops were held in readiness for the copper, and which shielded the hops from sunlight coming through the rooflights. This photosensitivity of hops is, supposedly, carried through to the finished beer. The reason for beer being traditionally supplied in dark bottles is to prevent the beer from becoming 'sunstruck', and not to hide its murky contents from the hapless imbiber, as is commonly believed.

On examination, the hops should be green in colour, perhaps yellowish if sulphured, but certainly not brown. They should be strong in aroma and sticky to the feel. You should, of course, observe how the hops have been stored and if any of the above criteria do not meet with your satisfaction – simply reject them.

Your hops can be stored on a short term basis by simply placing them in an air-tight, light proof container and placing them in the coolest place in the house. If your hops are supplied in a compressed block, do not be tempted to break open the block until you are ready to use them.

Hop pellets

Hop pellets have been around for perhaps a hundred years or more, but have not gained particularly wide acceptance. Hop pelletisation consists of removing unwanted debris, such as leaves and strings, from the hops and then milling the hops to a powder. The hop flour is then compressed under great pressure into solid round pellets of about half an inch in diameter by about 1 inch long. Hop pellets have a more stable storage characteristic than whole hops due to the pelletisation process preventing air from gaining access to its centre, only the outside of the pellet could be exposed to the atmosphere, but this is eliminated by vacuum packing the pellets or packing them in an inert nitrogen atmosphere. Hop pellets are of no use in a traditional brewhouse because the spent whole hops are used to provide a filter bed for the removal of trub from the boiled wort. Some breweries use hop pellets for dry hopping where they eliminate the need to remove the spent hops from the barrel during the subsequent cleaning and sterilisation operation.

Hop pellets could possibly be usefully employed by the home brewer, where their better storage characteristic may be an advantage. However, I have my doubts about hop pellets. I feel that they impart a harsh after-taste to beer, which gets worse with age. I find the taste objectionable, although many people don't.

Liquid hop extracts

Hop extracts have been around for a number of years, however some confusion exists among home brewers as to their proper application. There are two basic types of hop extract, one of these contains alpha-acids and is used to adjust the bitterness of the brew, and the other contains hop oils and is used to provide a 'hoppy' aroma. These two basic types are available in two forms, soluble and non-soluble. The non-soluble types are the extracts supplied in their raw state and should be mixed with the wort prior to boiling for proper utilisation. The other types have been specially processed to make them soluble in water and can be added to the beer at any stage of production. It is the soluble types that are most useful to the home brewer.

Hop aroma extracts and emulsions

Aroma extracts are extracts of hop oils which provide the hoppy aroma to beers. They do not impart bitterness. Hop aroma emulsions are these extracts in water soluble form. Hop aroma emulsions can be used at any stage of the brewing process, but it should be remembered that the essential oils of hops are volatile and will distill-off if they are subjected to a prolonged boiling period. Hop aroma extracts do not offer any advantages over dry hopping with whole hops as far as the home brewer is concerned, but they can be useful for making late corrections to aroma. Hop aroma extracts (non emulsified) are very potent, and in the undiluted form are added to beer at the rate of 1 or 2 parts per million. Hop aroma emulsions are somewhat less potent, but still require considerable care to be exercised if the desired aroma is to be achieved. Emulsions, as received from the manufacturers, are usually added to beer at the rate of 1 or 2 millilitres per 2.5 litres of beer, and the appropriate quantity needs to be accurately measured by means of a graduated syringe or pipette. The hop emulsions available via the home brew trade will have been diluted by a certain degree and the suppliers instructions should be carefully followed to obtain the correct dosage rate. Always use the most accurate form of measurement available to you – don't approximate – otherwise you will not obtain consistent results. Graduated syringes are available from chemists.

Isomerised hop extract

Isomerised hop extract is an extract of hops containing only the natural bittering components, converted into a water soluble form. The alpha-acids (humulones) have been converted by an industrial process into isohumulones. It is used to supply additional bitterness to beer and can be used at any stage of beer production. Isomerised hop extract should not be used as the sole source of hop products in the wort, this is because brewer's yeasts require some additional hop material to be present for proper behaviour. Isomerised hop extract is useful for making bitterness corrections to the finished beer, should it not turn out to be as bitter as intended.

Isomerised hop extract is very concentrated, and is very potent as it comes from the factory, but home brew suppliers invariably dilute it by at least 10:1 with deionised water before packaging. The exact dilution is dependant upon the supplier. Again, great care should be taken in using these extracts. It is very easy to ruin your beer by using too much. Read the supplier's instructions carefully before use, and again use the most accurate form of measurement available to you, such as a graduated syringe. Do not approximate if you want consistent results. Remember that once you have put it into the beer .... there ain't no way you're gonna get it out again.

The hop extract can be added at any stage of beer production but the most convenient place is probably in the fermenting vessel at the end of fermentation, where overall bitterness can be judged, and where it can be properly mixed into the beer. It can also be added directly to the barrels, along with the primings and a few dry hops if desired, but it should be added and mixed into the beer before finings are added.

Boiling hops in water

Malt extract brewers sometimes adopt the practice of boiling hops separately in water and then adding the water to the fermentation vessel. However, the bittering component of hops will only isomerise, that is become soluble in water, in the presence of certain metallic trace elements which act as catalysts. Although these trace elements may be present in sufficient quantities in the water to effect isomerisation, in the conventional brewing process these catalysts are generally supplied by the malt. In order to ensure complete isomerisation, half a teaspoonful of magnesium sulphate, and half a teaspoon of calcium sulphate should be added to the water prior to boiling. It is far better brewing practice for malt extract brewers to boil their hops with the malt extract, rather than boil them separately in water. However, the addition of the catalysts is still to be recommended whether one boils the hops with water or with the extract.

A traditional mash tun

7 Yeast

Yeast is probably the most important item used in the production of beer, yet its significance is often underrated. Of all of the books about home brewing that I have seen, not one of them, in my opinion, provides an adequate chapter on yeast. This lack of information gives the impression that yeast is of minor importance, and that 'any old yeast' will do! Unfortunately, that is not the case. It is not generally appreciated by the amateur brewer that about half of the components that go towards the flavour of beer are supplied by the yeast in the form of fermentation by-products. The quality, flavour, and aroma of a beer are all affected by the type and quality of the yeast employed. It is also not generally appreciated that there are several hundred different strains of yeast, some of which are unsuitable for beer making; but of those that are suitable for beer making, each one will impart different characteristics to the final beer.

Yeast and commercial breweries

Commercial breweries attach considerable importance to the quality and pedigree of their yeast strain. In bygone days there were as many as 8,000 breweries around the country. Most villages boasted at least one brewery, and modestly sized towns had several. All of the breweries in a particular town tended to use the same type of yeast, because, if by misfortune, a particular brewery's yeast had become contaminated or if it died out for any reason, the head brewer simply walked down the road to the next brewery and borrowed a bucket of yeast. The chances were that the other breweries were not suffering from the same problem at the time. It mattered not how fierce the rivalry may have been between the two breweries concerned, no self respecting brewer ever refused a competitor a fresh charge of yeast – it was an unwritten law. As a result of this practice, specialist strains of yeast were maintained for a great many years and were safe from extinction due to the fact that the same strain was being propagated independently by several different breweries.

In these more modern times when there are less than two hundred breweries still in existence, the ability to walk down the road for a fresh charge of yeast has long gone. To overcome this problem the breweries have collectively set up yeast banks. These are independent laboratories whose job it is to propagate, culture, and look after the different strains of yeast employed by the breweries around the country. It is very rare, in these days of modern scientific acumen for a large brewery to lose its strain of yeast, but should that happen the head brewer simply phones the yeast bank and orders a fresh yeast culture (and presumably someone somewhere gets a rocket!).

It is a pre-requisite of continued high profits to the brewery that the beer it produces should not suddenly change character. If a brewery was forced to change its yeast strain, the chances are that it would result in a considerable change in the character of its beer. Although it may still be high quality, palatable beer, which would be perfectly acceptable to a stranger in the area, to the locals it may taste quite different, and that could result in the brewery's established customers indignantly refusing to drink its product. The strain of yeast employed by any traditional commercial brewery has been bred, nurtured, pampered and coaxed over a period of many years to produce the type and character of beer which best suits its customers. The culture of yeast employed by any particular brewery may be a single germanic strain, it may be a mixture of several strains, or it may be a hybrid (a mongrel so to speak). The home brewer should place just as much importance on the quality of his yeast as the commercial brewer does.

Little animicules in your wort!

Yeast is a form of fungus. A single celled plant that has the ability to convert the sugars in our wort into roughly equal weights of alcohol and carbon dioxide. There are hundreds of different types of yeast, most of them are quite unsuitable for the production of beer. Brewer's yeasts generally fall into two categories: top working, whereby the yeast rises to the surface of the wort during fermentation; and bottom working, whereby the yeast falls to the bottom of the vat during fermentation. The type of yeast that is employed in the manufacture of traditional English beer is a top working class of yeasts given the generic name of Saccharomyces Cerevisiae. There are bottom working classes of Saccharomyces Cerevisiae but these are not used for English beers. A bottom working class of yeast is employed for the manufacture of continental style lagers which is given the generic name of Saccharomyces Carlsbergenis (now re-named as Saccharomyces Uvarum).

The group of yeasts classed as saccharomyces cerevisiae consists of a very large number of individual strains and some of these strains are again unsuitable for the production of good quality English beer. Each individual strain of yeast differs in its characteristics and each strain will impart different qualities to the finished beer; some desirable, some undesirable. The various strains of yeast also differ in other ways, such as the speed at which they ferment the wort, their ability to separate from the beer when fermentation is complete, the type of wort in which they prefer to work, their sugar tolerance, their alcohol tolerance and one hundred and one other things.

Heavy breathers!

Our pet yeast has two methods of respiration, **aerobic** (with oxygen), and **anaerobic** (without oxygen). Not all yeasts have the ability to respire by two different methods, but all brewer's yeasts have this ability. A brewer's yeast prefers to respire aerobically if given the opportunity, and will do so if the medium in which it is working has a plentiful supply of dissolved oxygen. However, when the supply of dissolved oxygen is used up, the yeast will revert to anaerobic respiration whereby it synthesizes its oxygen (in fact, not strictly true) from the medium in which it is working.

When the yeast is first pitched it respires aerobically utilising the dissolved oxygen in the wort. During this aerobic phase the yeast multiplies at an exponential rate and very quickly establishes itself. To ensure that this preliminary, rapid growth phase takes place, the brewer must ensure that the wort is well aerated before the yeast is pitched, because the yeast will only multiply significantly if it is permitted to respire aerobically. When the dissolved oxygen in the wort has been used up, the yeast is then forced to revert to anaerobic respiration. Reproduction noticeably slows down as the yeast adapts itself to anaerobic respiration. The yeast always finds it a bit of a struggle to respire anaerobically, but it is only under anaerobic conditions that alcohol is produced. There is absolutely no point in blowing air through your wort in order to maintain the oxygen level for the benefit of your yeast, although the yeast may approve of your thoughtfulness, it will not produce alcohol, and the resulting fluid will be quite unlike beer. In fact, apart from the initial aeration of the wort before the yeast is pitched, it is very important to ensure that air is not allowed to come into contact with the beer from that point onwards.

Sugars (carbohydrates)

Before we proceed any further with this discussion on yeast, it would be as well to include a little background on sugar. Yeast is only able to ferment sugars, but sugar is a very general term indeed, scientifically it has much wider domain than the stuff that we simply stir into our tea. There are many different sugars, or carbohydrates, which can be derived from a variety of materials. There are simple sugars such as fructose and glucose, and there are more complex sugars such as sucrose and maltose.

Sugars consist of carbon, hydrogen, and oxygen atoms, and all sugars are classified as to their complexity, and the number of carbon atoms per molecule that they contain.

Monosaccharides

Simple sugars are known as **monosaccharides** (single molecule sugars). The three monosaccharides that are of interest to us, as far as brewing is concerned, are:

Glucose, Fructose, and Galactose

All three of these simple sugars have the same general formula, $(C_6H_{12}O_6)$ and differ only in their structure. As can be seen from the formula, these simple sugars contain six carbon atoms per molecule and are thus known as **Hexose Monosaccharides**. Despite the name being somewhat of a tongue-twister, brewer's yeast is able to ferment all three of these sugars without difficulty. These simple sugars are the basic building blocks of the complex sugars. All complex sugars consist of two or more simple sugars bonded together molecularly.

Disaccharides

Disaccharides are sugars which consist of two monosaccharides with a molecular link, or bond between them. Common disaccharides and their component monosaccharides are:

> **Sucrose** (cane sugar) = Glucose + Fructose
> **Maltose** (malt sugar) = Glucose + Glucose
> **Lactose** (milk sugar) = Glucose + Galactose

These sugars have the general form $(C_{12}H_{22}O_{11})$ because a molecule of water (H_2O) has been given off in the bonding. Brewer's yeast is unable to ferment disaccharides directly; the molecular bonds, or links, between the two sugars must be broken first. As far as sucrose and maltose is concerned, the yeast secretes enzymes (invertase and maltase respectively) which break the sugar down into its two component parts. However, the yeast can not secrete an enzyme capable of breaking lactose into it's component parts, thus lactose is non fermentable, and can be used for the sweetening of beers. In fact lactose is the agent used for sweetening of stouts, and is the reason for the picture of a milk churn on the Mackeson label.

Polysaccharides and Oligosaccharides

The more complex sugars known as polysaccharides and oligosaccharides consist of a number of simple monosaccharides bonded together molecularly; oligo meaning few, poly meaning many. Starch is, in fact, a polysaccharide. During mashing, enymes attack the molecular bonds between the starch molecules and break the starch down into simpler sugars: maltose, maltotriose (a trisaccharide), and various dextrins. Dextrins are oligosaccharides, but brewer's yeast is not capable of breaking dextrin down into its component parts and is therefore unfermentable. Dextrin is responsible for the residual sweetness in beers.

It's the enzymes that do it!

The yeast does not convert the sugars in our wort to alcohol and carbon dioxide directly, but instead release enzymes (sort of biological catalysts) which do the work for it. The group of enzymes responsible for alcoholic fermentation are often called the **Zymase** complex, but that is an old fashioned name left over from a hundred years ago when brewing scientists thought that only one enzyme (Zymase) was responsible for alcoholic fermentation, in fact there are several which work together. Some of these enzymes break down the complex sugars in the wort (maltose) into simpler sugars such as glucose, others work on the simpler sugars.

When the yeast is deprived of atmospheric oxygen, it releases these specialist enzymes which are able to break down hexose sugars in the wort into their component parts, other oxidizing enzymes then act upon these components to synthesise the energy that the yeast needs to function. The yeast is able to respire without dissolved atmospheric oxygen because oxygen atoms are one of the component atoms of sugar. The alcohol and carbon dioxide that is produced is the result of the yeast and its enzymes changing the molecular structure of the sugars by removing certain components that the yeast needs to produce energy.

The major sugars that are to be found in our wort are, **maltose** (malt sugar), **sucrose** (cane sugar), and **dextrins**. The sugars are able to penetrate the cell wall with the aid of of a group of enzymes called **permeases.** Once within the cell maltose is acted upon by an enzyme called (surprisingly) **maltase**, this converts the maltose to glucose, which is readily assimilated by the yeast cell. Sucrose is acted upon by another enzyme called **invertase** which breaks down the sucrose into invert sugar which is a mixture of glucose, fructose, both of which are readily assimilated by the yeast cell. Some non fermentable sugars (dextrins) and some residual solids remain. The dextrins are a group of sugars that the brewers yeast is unable to attack, or is only able to attack very slowly. There are some strains of yeast that are able to ferment dextrins but they are not often used for brewing purposes because they are usually unable to ferment maltose. Some classes of beer (known as Lites) have in fact had the dextrins fermented down along with the other sugars, but this is achieved by adding a bacterium or an industrial enzyme to the wort during fermentation. This enzyme (**amyloglucosidase**) converts dextrins into glucose. The quantity of dextrins in our wort is determined by our grist make-up and by the mashing stage of our beer production. Once the sugars have been converted to suitable form and are within the yeast cell, the oxidizing enzymes begin work and break down the sugars into alcohol and carbon dioxide, and in so doing release energy for use by the yeast cell. Not all of the energy thus released is used by the yeast cell; the surplus energy causes the temperature of the wort to rise during fermentation.

Yeast reproduction

Not only does brewers yeast have two methods of respiration, but the crafty little blighters also have two methods of reproduction. The first of these methods is called budding and is similar to, but not the same as, simple cell division. Firstly a bud grows out of the side of the yeast cell, followed by the nucleus of the cell dividing into two, one half of the nucleus then goes into the bud which continues to grow until it is about half the size of the parent cell at which point it separates from it. Brewer's yeasts do not reproduce by simple cell division (although some other yeasts do), where firstly the nucleus of the cell divides into two, followed by the whole cell dividing into two, with one half of the nucleus in each of the daughter cells.

The second method in which our brewers yeast reproduces is a sexual method whereby two yeast cells merge into one (fusion), followed some time later by the cell dividing up into four small spores, the cell usually continues to reproduce by budding for some considerable time between fusion and sporulation, but eventually the spores are thrown. These spores are particularly hardy and can survive conditions which a full grown cell cannot. In times of hardship a yeast culture will sporulate as part of its survival mechanism, the resulting spores can remain inert for considerable periods of time.

Adaptability

Brewers yeast is extremely adaptable to the changing conditions in which it finds itself, one assumes that given the rapid speed at which it multiplies, minor evolutionary changes in its makeup are achieved relatively quickly. However, the yeast is not capable of sudden changes. A yeast that has spent the last few generations producing a light mild ale will object most strongly if it is suddenly plunged into the wort of a strong old ale. The yeast's cell shape, and wall thickness gradually change to take best advantage of the nutrients and minerals that it finds in a particular wort. The practice of brewers pitching one brew with yeast that is skimmed from the top of a previous brew is auto-selective and considerably aids the evolutionary process. This preferentially selects yeast which performs well in the type of beer that we are producing and which has adapted to the minerals and other nutrients that our water supply or wort composition provides. Yeasts that do not have sufficient alcohol tolerance, do not have sufficient flocculating power (the ability to clump together and rise to the surface when their usefulness is over), wild yeasts, or mutant strains; either die off, sink to the bottom or remain in suspension in the wort. Either way, these unwanted yeasts are not skimmed off, and therefore are not propagated.

Flocculating power

As I seem to have casually mentioned flocculating power in the preceding paragraph, it is fitting that some brief mention of the subject should be made here. During fermentation the active yeast is in suspension in our wort. When a yeast cell produces a molecule of alcohol it also produces a bubble of carbon dioxide gas, the yeast is carried up through the wort with the bubble until the bubble is released, whereby the yeast cell will sink back down through the wort collecting more nutrients and in turn producing a molecule of alcohol and another bubble of gas. Bearing in mind the speed at which yeast multiplies, if all of the yeast produced remained in suspension in the wort indefinitely, we would end up with a singularly turbid fluid that would taste quite unlike beer. Fortunately for us, brewers yeasts **Flocculate**. That is; when the yeast cells reach a particular age they form the ability to clump together and, in the case of top working yeasts, become buoyant (without the aid of Co_2) and rise to the surface of the wort where they remain until we remove them. A bottom working yeast will sink to the bottom after flocculation. A yeast strain that does not flocculate will remain in suspension in the wort. A strain that flocculates too young will ferment the wort at a slower rate because only the youngsters are in the wort doing the work while the middle aged and old men are sitting it out on the top (ie, the yeast concentration is lower). Fortunately for us, our yeast skimming method mentioned above selects yeast that flocculates to the degree that we require. Non flocculating types remain in suspension and are not selected. Early flocculating types do not remain in the wort for as long as the desired types and therefore do not have the opportunity to multiply to as great a number, and therefore, are unable to establish themselves to a harmful degree. As the fermentation progresses, and the wort pH decreases, the flocculating age of the yeast decreases. At the completion of fermentation most of the yeast should be on top or on the bottom of the vessel, depending upon strain, leaving us with a much lower concentration of yeast in the beer. The concentration of yeast remaining can be lowered further if desired by cooling after fermentation, which will cause the remaining yeast to settle on the bottom of the vessel; and/or by fining our finished beer. Different yeast strains have different powers of flocculation, and the flocculating power of individual yeasts is again affected by wort nutrients, wort pH, and temperature.

Fermentation by-products.

Besides producing alcohol and carbon dioxide there are many other compounds that are produced in small amounts by the fermentation process. It is these by-products of fermentation that are responsible for much of the taste, character and aroma of your favourite pint, and are often referred to as flavour compounds.

Some of these compounds are hydrocarbons and higher alcohols which go under the general name of fusel oils, other by-products are esters and organic acids. Different strains of yeast produce different fermentation by-products in varying quantities. Furthermore, the type and the relative quantities of these important compounds are affected by wort composition, fermentation temperature, and wort acidity (pH). Even the dimensions of the fermentation vessel are said to affect them! It is for this reason that one brewery may find it impossible to duplicate a beer from another, even though they may be using exactly the same recipe. It is also why a brewery places so much importance upon its strain of yeast. Some of the by-products of fermentation, such as methyl alcohol and acetaldehyde are undesirable in beer, but these disappear during the maturing stage. A wort that has been fermented at a too high temperature will usually produce a beer that has unpleasant off-tastes. This is due to the fact that different temperatures and pH will activate different enzymes, which in turn produce different by-products, some of which have unpleasant tastes and do not disappear during maturation.

Yeast nutrients

Yeast uses sugars, amino acids and peptides present in our wort as food, but the yeast also requires vitamins and minerals in the same way that we do. A properly balanced wort will normally supply all of the supplementary foods that the yeast requires. However, it is worth bearing in mind that cane or beet sugar does not contribute minerals to the wort. In fact, ordinary sugar is pure energy, nothing else. Unlike malt it does not supply the additional ingredients necessary to enable the yeast (or us for that matter) to convert its own energy into a useful form. These minerals have to be supplied from elsewhere. The major minerals required are nitrogen, phosphates and trace elements such as calcium and magnesium. Yeast, strangely enough, also requires vitamin B1, and most brewer's yeasts also require some hop products to be present in the wort for normal behaviour to occur. It is not fully understood why certain types of yeast require these hop products to be present, or indeed what particular substances it is that they require. It is probably the result of hundreds of years of training our yeast to actually like hopped beer, now it seems that it **insists** upon it. These hop products are produced when the wort is boiled with the hops, and is one reason why some yeasts do not perform well with home brew kits in which the hop flavours are provided by means of adding hop extracts, and not by boiling hops with the wort.

Some of the trace elements are used by the yeast cell directly, while others play a catalytic role (known as co-enzymes) in conjunction with the enzymes during the alcoholic reduction process. Sufficient trace elements will almost always be present in your wort. They are supplied by both the brewing water and the malt. It is possible, although very rare, to produce a wort that is deficient in nitrogen or phosphates. This is normally due to a poor recipe (too much sugar), or more likely over enthusiastic water treatment (too much calcium sulphate added). Should a wort be deficient in these compounds the situation can be remedied by adding two or three teaspoons of ammonium phosphate per five gallon batch. However, should your wort require the addition of supplementary foods for the benefit of your yeast, then there is something wrong with either your water treatment or your wort composition.

It is a common practice to put a yeast nutrient into the yeast starter to ensure that an abundant source of nutrient is readily available, although this should also be unnecessary.

A suitable composition for a full yeast food is as follows:

TABLE 7.1

30 parts	AMMONIUM PHOSPHATE	(nitrogen)
5 parts	POTASSIUM PHOSPHATE	(potassium)
1 part	CALCIUM PHOSPHATE	(calcium ions)
1 part	MAGNESIUM SULPHATE	(magnesium ions)
2 parts	POTASSIUM CHLORIDE	
2 parts	ANEURINE HYDROCHLORIDE	(vitamin B)

This can be pre-mixed in bulk and stored in an air-tight container. A pinch of the compound in the yeast starter, and/or a couple of teaspoons per five gallon batch is a more than sufficient dose. This nutrient supplies all of the needs of the yeast, in fact, it is possible to ferment cane sugar by adding this and some yeast to a sugar solution.

Selecting a yeast

The acquisition, care, and maintenance of our yeast is a matter of some considerable importance. We do not have the well equipped laboratory facilities or the trained chemists and microbiologists that are available to the commercial brewer. We need to take extra care at every stage of beer production, particularly where our yeast is concerned. One of the biggest problems facing the home brewer is that of maintaining consistent quality. It is not possible to produce consistently good, reproducible beer, if the yeast strain is not up to scratch.

It is almost impossible to recommend any particular type or source of yeast. A yeast that functions satisfactorily for one brewer may not be as successful for another. There are a number of things that affect yeast activity; water composition, wort composition, and pH. Also, different yeasts impart subtly different flavours to the beer. Different brewers have different preferences. A good yeast should contribute no undesirable flavours to the beer, should rapidly form a thick protective head during fermentation, should remain vigorous at temperatures down to about 16°C. (60°F.), and it should clear out of solution quickly after fermentation; packing down hard onto the bottom of the vessel. Some yeasts clear down so well that fining is unnecessary.

Many packaged yeasts, particularly dried yeasts, are of very dubious origin. Some packaged yeasts, particularly those supplied with beginner's beer kits, very often are not top working brewers yeasts at all, but a wine yeast. Never use anything other than genuine top working brewers yeast for ales, and a lager yeast for lagers. You should experiment with different sources of yeast until you find a yeast that suits both you and the type of beer that you are producing and stay with it.

Dried yeasts

Most dried yeasts supplied to the home brew trade are freeze dried. Freeze dried yeast may be perfectly okay for wine, lager, or bakers yeast, but not for ale yeast. In general, top working brewers yeast **Does Not Survive** the freeze drying process, only the spores are likely to survive. There are methods of drying brewers yeast, by first washing it to remove wort residues, pressing it in a hydraulic press to remove most of the moisture and then drying it by means of gentle heat, under vacuum. Yeast that has been gently dried has a different appearance from freeze dried yeast. Freeze dried yeast is composed of spherical granules of varying sizes, whereas the gently dried variety has the appearance of dirty flakes.

Yeasts in suspension

Yeasts supplied in suspension form are much better than dried yeasts, but you must ensure, for ales at least, that the label states that the yeast is a genuine top working brewer's yeast. Many yeasts that are simply called 'brewer's yeast' are very often a lager yeast. For home brew lagers I would still recommend using a top working yeast, but if you prefer to use a lager yeast make sure that the packet says that that's what it is.

Real live brewers yeast

The best way of ensuring that you have genuine top working brewers yeast, is to get it from a brewery; but you should ensure that the brewery concerned uses the open fermentation method. More and more breweries these days are going over to conical fermentors, and often use a specially 'trained' form of bottom working yeast for their purpose. Many home brew shops sell real live brewers yeast from a local brewery. However, do not be fooled into thinking that because you have obtained your yeast from a brewery that it MUST be good stuff. Some breweries' strains of yeast are quite temperamental and some need to be roused at regular intervals. The breweries tolerate the situation because their particular yeast imparts a flavour which they desire. As home brewers we normally do not have the time to continually watch over our beer, therefore, a yeast that requires frequent rousing is undesirable. Fortunately for us, the majority of R.L.B. yeasts are good, hard working, vigorous strains.

Taking yeast from a commercial beer.

Many home brewers start their yeast culture by taking yeast from a commercial LIVE bottled beer. Most bottled beers are pasteurised in this day and age which kills the yeast and makes it quite unsuitable for our purpose. At the time of writing, only two nationally available live bottled beers remain in existence, Worthington White Shield, and bottled Guinness (draught Guinness is a keg). Bottled Guinness sold in Scotland is pasteurised and is therefore unsuitable. Guinness yeast is superb and has been the work horse of the enthusiastic home brewer for donkey's years. The procedure is simple:

Go round to your local pub and bring home a bottle of Guinness, let it stand undisturbed for a day or so to allow the yeast sediment to settle. Having done this, carefully remove the cap and gently pour all but the last half of an inch of the contents of the bottle into a glass taking care to ensure that any sediment is undisturbed and remains in the bottle. Drink the contents of the glass.

Make up a yeast starter solution as detailed below, and when the starter solution has cooled to room temperature tip a quantity of the solution into the Guinness bottle and give it a very vigorous shake. Guinness yeast often packs down quite firmly onto the bottom of the bottle, the shake is an attempt to loosen this. Pour the contents of the Guinness bottle back into the starter bottle and check that there is no yeast left clinging to the bottom of the Guinness bottle. If there is, repeat the shaking operation. Fit an airlock, etc, as described below. In a few days time you should have a quantity of actively fermenting Guinness yeast. Guinness has a very low yeast count, therefore it can be a bit sluggish in starting.

Yeast starters

Yeast can be fickle stuff, particularly dried yeast. Before we begin a brew it is good practice for us to ensure that we have a sufficiently large quantity of actively working yeast to guarantee a rapid start to our main fermentation. We do this by producing a yeast starter culture a couple of days ahead of when we plan to brew. The time between pitching the yeast into our wort, to the yeast multiplying sufficiently to provide a protective head and begin fermentation, is a very dangerous period of our home brewing process. Brewers wort is a perfect culture medium, rich in all sorts of nutrients, vitamins and minerals. All manner of little 'nasties' are quite happy to breed in it, and will do so if they are given the opportunity. If a 'nasty' succeeds in establishing itself before the yeast does, then the chances are that our beer will be ruined. Obviously anything that we can do to give our yeast a head start can only be to our advantage. Furthermore, with yeast being the fussy creature that it is, it is as well to ensure that it is in the mood to perform for us before we commit it to five gallons of wort.

Yeast starter mediums are easy enough to make up, they are of course based upon brewers wort. The general procedure is as follows:

A SIMPLE YEAST STARTER

Sterilise a milk bottle and a small funnel using Chempro SDP or similar and rinse very thoroughly. Pre-heat the milk bottle by filling it with boiling water and leave it to stand.

In a small saucepan bring approximately 1/2 of a pint of water to the boil, add a tablespoon of sugar, and two tablespoons of malt extract. Continue to simmer gently for about a minute stirring continuously to avoid burning and then turn off the heat. At this point you can add a pinch or two of yeast nutrient if desired.

Empty the milk bottle and carefully pour the hot starter solution into the bottle via the funnel. Cover the mouth of the bottle with a piece of kitchen towel, or sterile cloth, secured with an elastic band, to reduce the possibility of airborne contamination while the solution is cooling. Stand the bottle in a bowl of cold water and leave to cool to room temperature.

When the solution has cooled to room temperature, cover the neck of the bottle and give the bottle a vigorous shake to admit oxygen into solution. We now have a starter medium which is just about as sterile as we can make it.

If you are using a packaged yeast, add the yeast to the starter bottle, give another vigorous shake, fit an airlock, and stand the bottle in a place where the temperature is suitable (18 to 20°C).

If you are taking yeast from a bottle of beer, follow the instructions given for Guinness above.

I make no apologies for unauthorised use of a milk bottle! A standard milk bottle is a good vessel for yeast starters, it is designed to withstand the temperature shocks described above, and it will accept a winemakers rubber bung and airlock, although some bottles will only accept the half gallon bung.

If you are fortunate enough to have access to a Pyrex flask, a more sterile method of producing a yeast starter medium is to add the water, malt extract, and sugar to the flask, and heat the flask directly, simmering the contents for about a minute. Cover the neck of the flask as above, and cool the flask under cold running water. When the flask has cooled to room temperature, add the yeast, shake, fit airlock etc.

In a matter of hours CO_2 bubbles should be produced and some time later the frothy head should start to appear. You should not begin to prepare your main brew until your yeast starter is properly established. If required, the starter can be left fermenting for a day or two until you are ready to brew the main batch. However, if you allow your yeast starter to go anaerobic, there will be a greater lag phase when the yeast is eventually pitched. It takes time for the yeast to change from anaerobic to aerobic respiration and vice-versa. Always give the contents of the bottle a good 'sniff', to ensure that it is sound, before using it. I have, in the past, found packaged yeasts to be contaminated with bacteria.

Propagating your own yeast

The majority of enthusiastic home brewers propagate their own yeast by saving some from one brew to start the next. This has the advantage that we maintain a yeast of known good performance for our own particular type of beer. This gives us a consistency that would be difficult to achieve if we relied completely on the whims of the packaging companies. Yeast that has been propagated on the same type of beer into which it is pitched should produce consistent results.

It is best to collect yeast for saving for re-pitching as late as possible into the beer making process; either from the surface of the wort towards the end of fermentation, or the bottom of our vessel after fermentation. By this time most of the alcohol has already been produced thereby ensuring that bacterial contamination has been checked. If you bottle your beers, then you can of course make a yeast starter from the dregs of a **recently** consumed bottle.

The first crop of yeast that forms on the surface of the wort is not suitable for repitching. The majority of this first crop has multiplied by utilising the dissolved oxygen in the wort (aerobic respiration), and has not even begun to think about producing alcohol. If we continually propagated our yeast using this crop we could end up with a variety of yeast that disliked alcohol! Furthermore, this first crop contains a high proportion of mutant cells, wild yeasts, bacteria, and it also contains solid particles and other non soluble matter carried up from the wort by the rising yeast. Likewise, the yeast sediment on the the bottom of the fermentation vessel is also unsuitable because this again contains mutant strains, bottom working varieties, dead cells, and yeast that, for one reason or another, has been unable to go all the way. Remember, for ale at least, we want a top working yeast, therefore yeast that is on the bottom of the vessel early in the fermentation process is in the wrong place! However, yeast that has sedimented in the bottom of bottles is okay. It is of good parentage. Its ancestry goes right back to pitching, and it has come all the way down the line to producing good beer. It is not advisable to use the dregs out of a barrel as a source of re-pitching yeast, particularly if you have allowed air to come into contact with the beer; the chances will be that bacterial contamination has already begun to set in. Your re-pitching yeast should always come from the strongest beers that you produce.

Storing yeast

There are several methods of storing yeast, but most home brewers are limited to storing their yeast by keeping it in the fridge or freezer. This method is fine for short term storage of about a week in the fridge, and several weeks or so in the freezer, but it is not really suitable for longer periods of time. The procedure is straight forward: If yeast is going to be stored in the fridge, remove as much beer residue as possible by drying the yeast using blotting paper or newspaper, mix the yeast into a slurry with fresh tap water in a suitable, sealable container. Label the container with the brew and date, place the container in the fridge. If your yeast is to be stored in the freezer; dry the yeast as much as possible, using a piece of blotting paper or newspaper. Squeeze it into a firm ball, wrap it in a piece of polythene and secure it with an elastic band. Label the package with the brew and date, and place it into a margarine tub. The yeast will keep longer if it is stored in the freezer, but freezing does damage the cells, and I suspect that it is only the spores that actually survive. Yeast starters made from frozen yeast are very slow to start.

Never re-use a yeast that has come from a brew that has been spoiled for any reason, or a yeast that looks discoloured or smells strange.

Recovering yeast from our own bottles.

Probably the most successful, and the best, amateur method of storing yeast on a long term basis, is to brew a special batch of beer specifically for yeast propagation purposes, and bottle it. The yeast will remain dormant in a bottle of sound strong ale for several years. Thousands of home brewers have propagated their yeast using this method, and have kept the same strain running for years.

The best type of ale to brew is a dark old ale of SG at least 1065, preferably higher, and the ideal time to brew is between November and March. Take extra precautions over cleanliness and sterilisation; I normally add about 60ppm of sulphur dioxide to these brews to ensure conditions alien to bacteria. A five gallon batch of this will provide upto 40 bottles of excellent beer which can be used to start a yeast starter medium as described above. The alcohol and sulphur dioxide will keep most problem forms of bacteria at bay.

Suspensions

Certainly the professional method of storing yeast is by placing it into a suspension medium. A suspension medium places the yeast into suspended animation by depriving it of certain nutrients and retarding osmosis. Yeast in suspension can be stored for many months without problems, furthermore, we can add antioxidants and antibacterial substances to keep the yeast relatively free from contamination. Because the yeast is not frozen, the cells are not damaged, and we have a more vigorous start to fermentation. A typical suspension medium consists of a solution in distilled or deionised water, of Mannitol or Sorbitol which retards osmosis thereby reducing the ability of the cell wall to assimilate certain nutrients. Sodium Metabisulphite can also be added which, apart from being antibacterial, is also an anti-oxidant and absorbs dissolved oxygen, which discourages aerobic forms of bacteria or yeast. Finally the solution can be acidified which will increase the effectiveness of the sulphur dioxide and destroy non acid tolerant bacteria. A suitable suspension medium is detailed below.

A SUSPENSION MEDIUM

Into 100 ml of distilled or deionised water containing about 100 ppm* of sulphur dioxide add 30 grams of Mannitol or Sorbitol and stir into solution. To this add a pinch of citric acid. Into this stir a couple of teaspoonfuls of fresh yeast and place into a suitable container having an air tight cap, pour a small amount of paraffin or light mineral oil onto the surface of the fluid and fit the airtight cap. Store upright in a refrigerator at about 4°C. The stirring operations should be performed gently. Do not shake to dissolve the ingredients because we do not want to admit any more air into solution than is absolutely necessary. To ensure that anaerobic conditions are maintained, a small quantity of paraffin, or light mineral is added to the solution; this will float on top of the medium, sealing it from the air.

When re using the yeast, the yeast is removed by inserting a syringe or pipette below the surface of the oil, and drawing the yeast into the syringe, leaving the oil behind. The yeast is filtered from the medium using a filter paper and then transferred to a yeast starter as above.

Bacterial contamination of yeast

One of the problems of propagating yeast by saving some from one brew to pitch a succeeding brew, is that bacteria can be transferred from brew to brew along with the yeast. Fortunately the home brew environment is such that, providing reasonable care is taken, catastrophic bacterial or wild yeast contamination of a brew is rare. Many home brewers have propagated the same yeast strain for many years without taking precautions against bacterial infection, and without suffering any noticeable contamination. The vast majority of wild yeasts, fungi, and bacteria are killed by the presence of alcohol and acids, both of which are present in the finished beer. Should a yeast strain become

* See chapter on making measurements

contaminated, it is best to obtain a fresh charge from your usual source. However, there may be a time when you wish to try to save a yeast which has become contaminated. Freeing yeast from contamination is never easy, but fortunately our brewer's yeast is fairly hardy stuff! Just look at this list of 'smarty points':

1). Brewer's yeast is able to respire by both aerobic and anaerobic mechanisms; wild forms of yeast and most forms of bacteria are either aerobic or anaerobic by nature; they can not change from one to the other.

2). Brewer's yeast uses sugar as its carbon source; some of the most troublesome forms of bacteria use alcohol as their carbon source.

3). One particularly troublesome form of bacteria requires a carbon dioxide atmosphere; Brewer's yeast doesn't give a monkey's what the atmosphere is.

4). Brewer's yeast is very tolerant (but not immune) to sulphur dioxide; many forms of wild yeast and bacteria are killed by it.

5). Brewer's yeast is very tolerant to alcohol; most wild yeasts and some kinds of bacteria are killed by it.

6). Brewer's yeast is very tolerant to mineral acids; most wild yeasts and almost all bacteria are killed by it.

Here is a list of possible solutions:

Items 1, 2, and 3.
By growing our yeast in a culture medium under aerobic conditions, either by blowing filtered air through the medium using a fish tank aerator, or by continually aerating the medium every few hours by other means, we will grow our yeast in conditions which are unfavourable to some types of bacteria. A very low level of alcohol will be produced, thus those forms of yeast that can only use alcohol as a carbon source will not be able to multiply to any great extent; likewise there will be no carbon dioxide atmosphere. This will not necessarily kill the susceptible bacteria, but it will reduce its ratio.

Item 4
By adding sodium metabisulphite to a yeast slurry, or a culture medium so as to produce about 200 ppm sulphur dioxide, most forms of bacteria will be killed on contact. After a standing period of an hour or more the yeast should then be filtered and recultured.

Item 5
By using the yeast to brew a very strong beer, say O.G. 1080, the high level of alcohol produced will check or kill most forms of bacteria. Adding sodium metabisulphite to produce about 60 ppm of sulphur dioxide **after the yeast**

has gone anaerobic should put paid to most other forms of bacteria, and yet allow the yeast to continue to thrive. The beer can be bottled and left for as long as is desired.

Mineral acid washing

Acid washing is the most successful method of freeing yeast from bacteria. It is in fact the first remedy that a commercial brewery would perform.

To acid wash, the yeast is mixed into a slurry with water. 70% phosphoric acid, or sulphuric acid is carefully added until the pH of the solution is about pH2 – pH2.5. The solution is allowed to stand for 4 or 5 hours. After the standing period the yeast is removed from the solution by means of a filter paper and immediately re-propagated.

Bearing in mind that the acids concerned are nasty corrosive substances, I would not recommend this approach to the amateur at all. If you must do it, use the utmost care. Wear safety glasses. Always add the acid to the slurry, never the other way round. Stir continuously while adding the acid. Any spillages or splashes on your person should be washed with copious quantities of water, and then neutralised with a strong solution of baking powder, bicarbonate of soda, or washing soda.

Other problems with yeast

There are several problems that can interfere with our yeast's ability to ferment our wort. The most common problem is that some types of yeast inherently flocculate early and require frequent **rousing**, that is, stirring the yeast back into the wort every twelve hours or so. Some commercial breweries deliberately use a yeast which requires rousing because it provides a flavour which the brewery desires. But as home brewers we do not usually have the time to be continually rousing our yeast, and are better off using a strain of yeast that does not require frequent rousing. If you are using a yeast that requires rousing, stirring the yeast back into solution every ten hours or so is all that is required.

Jekyll and Hyde

One of the most unfortunate characteristics of yeast, particularly hybrid strains, is its ability to suddenly mutate, ie, revert back to one of its parent strains. Even strains that are believed to be germanic can suddenly mutate due to the fact that somewhere in the distant past its ancestors had a bit of 'nookey' with an alien. This is a recessive gene problem, and there 'ain't' nothing that we can do about it. Only one yeast cell needs to mutate into one of its parents, or one stray cell find its way into the flock, and subsequently introduce a different genetic dominance in the offspring, for the whole flock to almost instantly mutate into the dominant form. The yeast multiplies so quickly that a genetic dominance very rapidly takes over the whole colony.

One of the problems facing brewers that use a hybrid yeast strain, is the increased risk of a mutation or a reversion to one or the other of the parent forms. In fact some hybrid yeast strains have a known life span of a certain number of generations before they automatically revert to one of the parent strains, the hybrid strain then needs to be re-cultured by cross breeding from the two original germanic parent strains. This is similar to F1 and F2 hybrid plants in the gardening world.

Unfortunately there is not much we amateurs can do if our strain of brewer's yeast becomes contaminated with a different strain of brewer's yeast, or if a hybrid strain mutates. Such manipulations require specialist laboratory facilities.

A commercial technique of obtaining a pure yeast culture is to heavily dilute the yeast in sterilised water and then to smear the resultant fluid onto a sterile wort agar medium contained in a dish. After incubation, isolated colonies of yeast will grow. A colony is selected and a few cells are transferred to a small quantity of sterilised water by means of a sterile wire and this is again smeared onto a wort agar medium. By repeating this operation as many times as necessary, it is possible by this method of repeated dilution, to obtain a colony of yeast that has grown from a single parent cell. Microscopic examination will serve to confirm that bacteria is not present. This technique is simple enough to be employed by the amateur, but you must be really keen!

Yeast weakness

Yeast weakness is a euphemistic term that is employed in the brewing world to describe a common condition whereby the yeast suddenly loses its power to ferment the wort, ie, the fermentation velocity or the fermentation efficiency suddenly decreases for no apparent reason. Yeast weakness covers a multitude of different ailments. It is difficult for the home brewer to determine which of the different possibilities is the real cause of the problem. Yeast weakness can, of course, be caused by a mutation as described above. It can be caused by a wild yeast straying into the colony and either becoming established or changing the genetic makeup of the bulk. A further problem with wild yeast contamination, is the fact that certain strains of yeast produce components called zymocides which serve as poisons to other strains of yeast and retard their fermenting powers or even kill them off completely. It is now known that certain viruses can attack yeast and actually make it ill. Sometimes a yeast can lose its ability to respire anaerobically, but still be able to respire aerobically. Of course the problem may not be due to a yeast weakness at all. It could be caused by incorrect fermentation temperature, acidity, or nutrient deficiency, although this is unlikely if a similar brew has been successfully made previously. It is also possible, although unlikely if the normal precautions are taken, that a bacteria has succeeded in establishing itself to the detriment of the yeast. If your yeast is apparently suffering from a yeast weakness try rousing the yeast, if that fails re oxygenate the wort by pouring it from one container to another, if that fails throw the brew away and obtain a fresh charge of yeast.

Fermenting vessels

8 Water and water treatment

'The water should be soft by all means. That of brooks and rivers is best. That of a pond, fed by a rivulet, or spring, will do very well. Rainwater, if just fallen, may do; but stale rainwater, or stagnant pond-water, makes the beer flat and difficult to keep; and hard water, from wells, is very bad it does not get the sweetness out of the malt, nor the bitterness out of the hops, like soft water; and the wort of it does not ferment well, which is certain proof of its unfitness for the purpose.'
William Cobbett, Cottage Economy, 1821

During the 'Pale Ale revolution', in the mid nineteenth century, it very soon became apparent that certain brewers had a reputation for brewing better quality pale ales than others. It did not take very long for the brewers to conclude that this was due to the differing mineral content of the water supplies available in the various areas.

It is true that the mineral content of brewing water is an important factor in the brewing process, but the suitability of various water supplies for brewing has been the subject of much myth, and misconception over the years; not only in the home brewing field, but, surprisingly, in commercial brewing as well.

Sources of water

All of our water comes to us in the form of rain. As it falls to earth it picks up quantities of atmospheric gases and pollutants which acidify it slightly. The most significant of these acids being carbonic acid which is produced by the admission of atmospheric carbon dioxide into solution. This acidified rainwater falls to earth, drains through the topsoil, percolates through mineral substrata and porous rock below the soil, through cracks and fissures in non porous rock, and finally settles onto a table of impervious rock where it waits to be collected. Alternatively it may overflow into a river, or surface as a spring. On its journey through the earth the water absorbs mineral salts. The type and quantity of these mineral salts absorbed is dependant upon the type of rocks and terrain through which the water passes before being collected.

Rainwater which falls onto sedimentary rocks will absorb minerals on its journey through the earth. Some of these minerals are directly soluble in water, whereas others need to react with the carbonic acid collected from the atmosphere to cause a chemical change in order to affect solubility.

Rainwater which falls onto insoluble rock such as slate or granite does not have the opportunity to pick up mineral salts and remains more or less mineral free. This water we know as soft water.

The most important minerals that are found in our water supplies in various proportions are as follows :

Calcium Bicarbonate, $Ca(HCO_3)_2$, now usually called calcium hydrogen carbonate, is one of the principle substance causing hardness in our water supplies, and is derived from calcium carbonate (common chalk). Calcium carbonate is insoluble in water, but in regions where there is a large proportion of calcium carbonate in the rock, the carbonic acid in the rainwater reacts chemically with the carbonates to produce soluble calcium **bi**carbonate.

Bicarbonate hardness is termed temporary hardness, because upon heating the bicarbonate is broken down into carbon dioxide, water, and calcium carbonate, which being insoluble will settle out.

The presence of bicarbonate ions in our water has a detrimental effect on the quality of our ale. Bicarbonate ions interfere with the fermentation process, buffer and reduce the effect of the more important sulphate ions, and mess up fining systems. Most commercial breweries take steps to ensure that their bicarbonate hardness is reduced to less than 20 ppm.

Calcium Sulphate, CaSO4, is another of the principle substances causing hardness in some water supplies and is a very important mineral as far as we brewers are concerned. Calcium Sulphate hardness is termed permanent hardness because it is not thrown out of solution upon boiling. Unlike calcium bicarbonate, this is an extremely beneficial mineral to our brewing process. It reacts with other components in the mash, causing phosphates to precipitate, which releases phosphoric acid and therefore acidifies the wort (lowers its pH). All the brewing processes benefit from the presence of calcium sulphate and a low mash pH; keeping qualities are improved, clarity is improved, trub formation is improved, hop extraction is improved, astringent flavours are buffered, and yeast is more vigorous. Whether we are able to notice these improvements in the home-brewing environment is a matter of conjecture, but anyway; that's the theory.

Calcium Sulphate acts as a buffer and tends to suppress harshness in an ale. This means that a high level of hops can be used to provide a full hop flavour and aroma, without extracting an undesirable harshness from other resins contained in the hops. Calcium ions are required by certain enzymes during mashing. If used in excess it will impart a harsh bitter taste to the ale. A further detrimental effect of using it in too high a quantity is the risk of precipitating polypeptides, polyphenols, and hop resins out of the ale. Calcium sulphate is commonly known as Gypsum.

Magnesium Sulphate, $MgSO_4 7H_2O$, is one mineral that sets the water of Burton upon Trent apart from the rest of the country. The water of Burton upon Trent has a relatively high level of Magnesium Sulphate when compared with the water of other areas. Magnesium is an important mineral required by the yeast during alcoholic fermentation, and magnesium sulphate provides the mineral in a permanent form, ie it will not precipitate out of solution upon boiling. Magnesium sulphate is said to have beneficial effects upon wort stabilisation during the boiling phase of our ale production. Magnesium sulphate does not have the same effect upon reducing the mash pH as does calcium sulphate and can not really be used for wort pH adjustment. Magnesium sulphate is more commonly known as Epsom salts, well known for providing inner cleanliness.

Sodium Chloride, NaCl, common salt. London water contains a relatively high proportion of sodium chloride (common salt). London was famous for its porters and stouts. Because of this, many home brewers claim that a high proportion of sodium chloride is necessary to produce dark ales, mild ales and stouts. Unfortunately this is a myth that seems to have been propagated by popular belief over the years. There is no scientific benefit to be gained during mashing, fermentation, etc, by the presence of salt in the water. There are however, some flavour advantages to be gained, as we can all imagine from our culinary experiences. Salt is known to act as a flavour enhancer and contributes fullness and mouthfeel to the ale. However, it is not absolutely necessary to add the salt directly to the water, you could probably add it your pint pot! I have an old recipe where instructions are given to add salt to the fermentation vessel after the first yeast skimming.

Why treat our water?

The primary reason for treating our water is to ensure that the pH of our mash is appropriate to the type of ale being brewed. Although our water authorities are obliged to give us water of good drinking quality, they are not obliged to give us water of good brewing quality! Modern water supplies contain purposely added chlorine or fluorides, plus increasing levels of stray synthetic chemicals, and the by-products of fertilisers and pesticides; even the birth pill hormone can be detected in London water supplies!

Traditionally, brewing water was treated in order to make its composition similar to that of Burton upon Trent, a process known as Burtonising. Nowadays water treatment consists of removing as much of the carbonate content of the water as possible and adding sulphates to lower the the mash pH.

Is water treatment necessary?

Probably not! No water is perfect for brewing, but the truth is that most hard water supplies in Britain will produce acceptable ales without treatment. A very large number of home-brewers produce high quality acceptable ales without bothering about water treatment, and so indeed do a good number of commercial breweries. There were, and still are, a large number of breweries all over the country, using dozens of different water sources, that have very high reputations for the quality of their pale ales. Conversely, of the 40 breweries that were located in Burton upon Trent at one time, only a handful of them had a reputation for brewing high quality pale ales. Although it is true that the water of Burton upon Trent is excellent for brewing pale ales, there is a lot more to brewing than the water supply. Indeed, even the water at Burton is not ideal. The success of Burton upon Trent as a brewing centre had far more to do with skill, excellent communications, and entrepreneurship than its water supply.

However, most ales can be improved by treating the water; although the only treatment necessary may be limited to boiling the water prior to brewing. I am of the opinion that all water used for brewing should at least be boiled to drive off purification chlorine/fluorine, which could taint the ale. Boiling also has the advantage that complete sterility is ensured and that unwanted calcium bicarbonate is precipitated.

It is probably not necessary to treat water when brewing from malt extract because the critical mashing stage has already been performed. However, the boiling of hops requires the presence of magnesium and calcium ions to effect isomerisation of the alpha-acids. If no water treatment is being performed, then, as a precaution, the addition to the hop boil of half a teaspoonful of magnesium sulphate, and half a teaspoonful of calcium sulphate, or alternatively, a teaspoonful of a proprietary Burton water treatment salts will ensure isomerisation.

Removal of calcium bicarbonate

No ale benefits from having bicarbonates present. In hard water areas the first task in any water treatment procedure is the removal of excessive calcium bicarbonate. Calcium bicarbonate can be reduced by boiling and this is the most popular method as far as home brewing is concerned. This simply entails boiling the brewing water for a few minutes, and then allowing it to stand for a while to enable the insoluble calcium carbonate to settle out. The water is then carefully transferred to a secondary container leaving the precipitate behind. Ensure that the water is well aerated before boiling takes place; a high level of dissolved oxygen helps drive off the CO_2 evolved in the process. Some breweries blow air through the water during the boil. Fresh mains water will usually contain a sufficient level of dissolved oxygen, particularly if the vessel is filled using some sort of spray nozzle or sparkler.

Another method of removing calcium bicarbonate is to add 0.1N sulphuric acid to the water to precipitate carbonates. Breweries favour the sulphuric acid treatment because it saves on time, energy, and increases vessel utilisation by eliminating the need to boil the water.

Burtonising

Burtonising is a term applied to water treatment, originally meaning making the water appropriate to that of Burton upon Trent, but in a more modern sense all forms of brewing water treatment are known as Burtonising.

A typical Burtonised water will have the following composition in ppm (mg/l):

TABLE 8.1

Calcium Ca	Magnesium Mg	Sodium Na	Sulphate SO$_4$	Chloride Cl	Bicarbonate HCO$_3$
294	24	24	801	36	0

Table 8.2 shows the additions required to 1 litre of SOFT water to achieve the figures shown in Table 8.1

TABLE 8.2

		Ca	Mg	Na	SO$_4$	Cl	HCO$_3$
1000 mg/l	Calcium Sulphate	294	—	—	705	—	—
150 mg/l	Magnesium Sulphate	—	24	—	96	—	—
60 mg/l	Sodium Chloride	—	—	24	—	36	—
		294	24	24	801	36	0

In almost all cases there will already be minerals present in the water. If the above treatment is added to hard water, there will be a respective increase in the mineral content. However, the additions shown above are a good starting point for any water treatment irrespective of water type.

Preliminary water treatment

Bring 25 litres of water to the boil and when it has been boiling for a couple of minutes, add:

25 g Calcium Sulphate (about 4 heaped teaspoons)
4 g Magnesium Sulphate (about 1 level teaspoon)
Sodium Chloride (common salt) to taste.

When the water has cooled, rack it off into a separate container leaving the precipitate behind.

If after a trial brew with this treatment you find that the pH of your mash is too high, then add more calcium sulphate when you next brew. If the pH is too low then add less calcium sulphate. Keep adequate records and eventually you will devise a water treatment that is appropriate for your needs.

Different types of ale may require different water treatments; grists that contain a large proportion of roasted malts will be naturally more acidic than those that don't. There is no real point in adjusting the magnesium sulphate content to be much different to that specified. The magnesium is a co-factor, or co-enzyme, and the water only needs to contain an adequate supply of magnesium ions; one or two teaspoonsful is ample.

Common salt is a matter of taste. It is said that dark ales and milds benefit from a higher quantity of salt. Typical quantities vary from about half a teaspoon for pale ale, to two and a half teaspoons for a stout, per 25 litre batch.

A Burtonisation formula used by most commercial breweries prior to world war two is shown in Table 8.3.

TABLE 8.3

For 25 litres batch

Potassium Sulphate	9g
Magnesium Sulphate	6g
Magnesium Chloride	5g
Sodium Chloride	13g
Calcium Chloride	18g
Calcium Sulphate	51g

The general procedure is the same as in the water treatment above. For milds and stouts the calcium sulphate is usually omitted. Again adjustments to pH if required should be made with calcium sulphate.

Table 8.4 shows the most important compounds found in, or added to our water, and their breakdown expressed as a percentage of their weight. As an example; 100 mg of Calcium Sulphate added to a quantity of water will add 29mg of calcium and 75mg of sulphate. If the same quantity is added to 1 litre of water it will increase the calcium content by 29 ppm and the sulphate content 75 ppm.

TABLE 8.4

Calcium Bicarbonate contains	24.8% Ca and 75.2% HCO_3
Calcium Sulphate contains	29.5% Ca and 70.5% SO_4
Magnesium Sulphate contains	16.2% Mg and 63.9% SO_4
Sodium Chloride contains	39.3% Na and 60.7% Cl
Calcium Carbonate contains	40.0% Ca and 60.0% CO_3

Blowing a myth

Almost all home brewing books published to date instruct the home brewer to add precipitate of chalk to his water when making dark ales and stouts. Apart from the fact that no ale will benefit from indiscriminately chucking handfuls of carbonate into the water; Precipitate of Chalk, will immediately precipitate out again! Calcium Carbonate is insoluble in water, unless, of course, one is prepared to blow carbon dioxide gas through his water.

I don't know why this myth began, or who was responsible for it, but almost every home brewing book that I have seen contains similar instructions. It began sometime in the 1960's, and, it seems to me, that just about every home brew author has copied this mistake ever since. In a recent home-brew book the author stated that stouts **like** a bit of bicarbonate hardness. This is absolute rubbish! Take it from me, *No beer likes bicarbonates.* Bicarbonates are alkaline; our mashing and fermentation processes prefer acidic conditions. It is ironic that over 170 years ago, William Cobbett knew that 'hard water, from wells' was bad for brewing, and yet there are books published in the late 1980s that say otherwise.

9 Mashing and sparging

'The auspicious moment approaches for the celebration of the nuptials between the malt and the water, the arena of the ceremony being the mash-tub, and the officiating high priest being a ferocious instrument known as the 'porcupine'. .... It is armed with long wooden teeth which have a peculiarly searching manner of their own, the contemplation of which is most eligible at a little distance'
From 'A GLASS OF PALE ALE' 1872, Courtesy of The Bass Museum.

Mashing is the process whereby the fermentable sugars are extracted from our malt and other grains. In the simplest possible terms, the mash consists of steeping our brewing ingredients in hot water at a carefully maintained temperature (of about 65°C) and allowing it to stand for up to two hours. During this standing period, the enzymes produced by the pale malt, convert the starch contained in the pale malt and in the other ingredients, into various types of sugar.

'Wots 'n enzyme ?'

An enzyme is the biological form of a catalyst, in that its presence is required as a link in the chain of events that comprise a particular biological action. Enzymes are an important part of any biological process, and are utilised by plants, and animals to perform particular functions. Different enzymes perform different functions. During mashing enzymes convert starch, which is a complex sugar, into simple sugars. Most of these sugars will be fermentable by the yeast; but some will be non fermentable.

In the true sense of the word; an enzyme, as in a catalyst, is not actually consumed during the particular biological process. When the particular process that the enzyme performs is complete, the enzyme is released to do more work elsewhere. However, in mashing, certain enzymes are forced to operate at the top of their temperature tolerance, which has the effect of giving them a short active life before they are destroyed by the heat. This is not normally a problem because replacement enzymes are usually continually unlocked as part of the process being performed.

There are a number of enzymes at work during our mashing process and they are known collectively by the old fashioned term of **diastase** complex enzymes. There are two **diastatic** enzymes in which we are particularly interested. The first of these is called **alpha-amylase**, which converts the starch in our malt into maltose, and dextrins. The second enzyme is called **beta-amylase,** which converts starch into maltose only. Maltose is a sugar that is fermentable by our yeast, whereas dextrin is a group of sugars which are non fermentable by our yeast and remain in the finished beer to provide residual sweetness and body. Beta-amylase is also able to attack some of the dextrins produced by the alph-amylase and break these down into maltose, but this effect is slow and not very pronounced.

Mash temperature and pH

All enzymes are very fussy about the conditions under which they will work. They are particularly sensitive to temperature and acidity (pH). Our pet enzymes are no exception. Alpha-amylase prefers a temperature of about 70°C and a pH of about 5.6, whereas beta-amylase prefers a temperature of about 60°C and a pH of about 5.0. Typical mash temperatures range from 60°C to 68°C and mash pH ranges from about 5 to 5.6, but pH 5.1 to pH 5.3 is typical. At lower temperatures than their optimum both enzymes still perform, but at a slower rate, which is in accord with most chemical and biological processes. However, at higher temperatures than their optimum the enzymes become progressively deacti-vated. Alpha-amylase begins to become deactivated at temperatures above about 70°C, and beta-amylase begins to become deactivated at temperatures above about 62°C. At temperatures above these the enzyme's life is progressively reduced, until at some particular temperature, the enzyme is destroyed immediately it is produced and cannot perform any useful work. Regarding pH sensitivity, the enzymes are not destroyed or deactivated over the range of pH values likely to be encountered in our mashing process, but they work faster and more efficiently at their optimum value.

As you will by now be aware, the pH and temperature of the mash has an important bearing upon mash reactions in as much as the relative speed at which the two important enzymes operate is affected to a large extent by differing pH and temperature values. There are a number of other important reactions taking place during our mash alongside the conversion of starch into sugars, some of these reactions are due to enzymes, others are due to other biological or chemical processes. All contribute to the flavour and stability of the finished beer in one way or another, and all are affected by temperature and pH.

Control of Fermentability

An important aspect of mashing is that we have control over the ratio of fermentable to non fermentable sugars in our wort, ie the fermentability. A wort containing a high proportion of non fermentable dextrins would be of low fermentability and would yield less alcohol than a high fermentability wort, but the beer would have more body and a higher level of residual sweetness. The opposite is true of a wort which contains a low proportion of dextrins.

To recap upon what we know so far: An enzyme; alpha-amylase, converts the starch in our malt into a group of non fermentable sugars known as dextrins, then (or alongside this) another enzyme; beta-amylase, converts starch and dextrins into a fermentable sugar known as maltose. We also know that alpha-amylase is quite happy to work over our temperature range of 60°C to 70°C, but that it works slowest at 60°C and low pH levels, and that it works fastest at 70°C and high pH levels. We also know that beta-amylase works fastest at around 60°C and at low pH values, but is progressively deactivated at temperatures above this. It should now be apparent that by messing around with temperature and pH, we are able to control the speed at which one enzyme works relative to the other, and thereby control the ratio of maltose to dextrin in our wort.

It then follows that if we are able to slow down the activity of beta-amylase relative to alpha-amylase, and then stop the mash before all of the dextrose is converted to maltose, we would have a wort containing a high proportion of non fermentable sugars, resulting in a sweet beer after fermentation.

Conversely if we provided optimum conditions for beta-amylase activity, slowed down the alpha-amylase activity, and permitted ample time for as much of the dextrose as possible to be converted into maltose, we would have a dry beer. However, in practice, we will always have a certain degree of residual sweetness remaining in our wort, because not all of the dextrins produced by the alpha-amylase are open to attack by beta-amylase. Furthermore, apart from supplying residual sweetness, dextrins also supply a certain amount of body and flavour to the finished beer. A beer that is brewed to be very dry could be of a rather thin taste.

The range of mash pH over which acceptable results will be obtained ranges from about pH 4.5 to about pH 5.6, where pH 4.5 tends to produce a dry beer, and pH 5.6 tends to produce a sweet beer. It is normal British brewing practice to provide a mash pH of about 5.3 and to control fermentability by means of the mash temperature, only lowering the pH if a drier beer is required than can be obtained from temperature adjustments. If a very dry beer is required it may be necessary to lower the pH to a value close to pH 4, and it may be necessary to add lactic acid to the mash to achieve this value. High mash temperatures favour the extraction of high molecular weight nitrogenous compounds, which although can be haze forming if present in too large a proportion, provide good flavours and head retention.

Table 9.1 shows optimum conditions for various degrees of fermentability. Remember that a high temperature and/or a high pH favours a sweet beer and a low temperature and/or a low pH favours a dry beer. Any combination of temperature and pH can be used to control the fermentability of your beer, ie, a mash at a pH of 5.3 and a temperature of 69°C will produce a sweeter beer than

TABLE 9.1 Typical mash conditions

	Temp.(°C)	pH	Dextrins	Mash Time
Limits	60 to 70	4.2 to 5.7		S.E.P. to 2.5 hours
Low F.	67 to 69	5.4 to 5.7	26%	S.E.P. to 1 hour
Typical	64 to 67	5.1 to 5.4	21%	1 to 1.5 hours
High F.	61 to 64	4.2 to 5.1	17%	1.5 to 2.5 hours

Low F. = low fermentability
S.E.P. = starch end point

a mash at the same pH and a temperature of 61°C. It is worth bearing in mind that a low mash temperature slows down the overall mash reactions to a certain degree, and this contributes to the longer mash times advocated for drier beers. It is also possible to use a combination of temperatures. Some commercial breweries begin the mash at 62°C, but about half way through they raise the temperature to 68°C by letting in hot water, and the mash is completed at this higher temperature.

Mash times

This conveniently brings another aspect of control into focus, namely, mash time. Mash times typically vary from about one-and-a-half hours to about two-and-a-half hours, depending upon the type beer being produced. During the latter part of the mash all of the starch has been converted to dextrin, and the beta-amylase is engaged in converting the dextrose into maltose. Given a sufficiently long mash time the maximum amount of dextrin would be converted to maltose, but this is, of course, undesirable if we are producing a sweetish beer. It is, therefore, obvious that the mash should be stopped as soon as the desired point has been reached. In fact, irrespective of the type of beer being produced, it is desirable to keep the mash time to the minimum necessary to achieve the desired result. This is because tannin is being extracted from the malt alongside our sugar conversion. An excess of tannin will produce a bitter off-taste in our ale, similar to that of stewed tea. Over-mashing, and more importantly over-sparging, may extract an undesirable level of tannin from the goods in the mash.

Under no circumstances should you resort to the practice of overnight mashing as advocated by some members of the home brewing fraternity. Apart from producing a particularly dry beer, this practice favours the extraction of tannins and other undesirable compounds from the malt. On the other hand, under-mashing can result in some of the starch contained in the malt not being fully converted. and this will result in a cloudy beer being produced. Fortunately there is a simple test that we can perform on our mash, namely the iodine starch end point test, which will tell us when all of the starch has been converted into sugar.

The starch end point test is straight forward. Place a very small amount of sweet wort from the mash onto a white dish or saucer, then, using a dropper place a drop of tincture of iodine onto the wort. If the iodine immediately turns a deep blue-black, starch is still present, if not, it isn't − simple.

If a dry beer is being produced, a sufficient length of time should be allowed after starch end point to ensure that all of the convertible dextrin has been converted into maltose. If a sweet beer is being produced, the mash should be stopped fairly soon after starch end point has been reached. An average mash time is about one and a half hours, although the starch end point may well have been reached within 20 minutes.

Stopping the mash

When a very sweet beer is being produced it is sometimes desirable to stop the mash when the desired mash time has been reached, otherwise the conversion of dextrins into maltose can continue past the desired point, thereby producing a drier beer than was intended. This is particularly important if a long period of time is likely to elapse between the completion of the mash and the boiling phase. Bearing in mind that the run-off and sparging operation after the mash can take up to two hours, it can be seen that a considerable amount of additional conversion can take place during this period. Stopping the mash simply entails rapidly raising the temperature of the mash to about 75°C, which has the effect of disabling the beta-amylase, thereby preventing any further conversion of dextrin into maltose, but it still enables the alpha-amylase to continue the conversion of any residual starches into dextrin, which otherwise could cause a haze to be formed in the finished beer. Another reason for raising the temperature of the mash is to assist liquifaction by reducing the wort viscosity and making mash tun run-off easier. The classic way of stopping the mash is to add hot water to the mash until the desired temperature has been reached, but with home brewing equipment this runs the danger of over diluting the wort, causing the boiler to be too full after sparging. Another method of stopping the mash is to fit a low wattage heater to the mash tun, and raising the temperature by means of this. However, the practice of stopping the mash can be considered advanced home brewing, and in any case, stopping the mash by these means can be regarded as unnecessary for most beers. Sparging with water maintained at about 77°C and collecting the sweet wort in the brewing boiler set to maintain the same temperature is usually sufficient.

Mash stiffness

There is another aspect of the mash which, surprisingly, has an effect upon the fermentability of our wort, and that is mash **stiffness**, ie, the ratio of grist to liquor. Thinner mashes have the effect of producing a wort of higher fermentability than does a stiffer (thicker) mash. However, the effect of this parameter is so small with respect to the others that for our practical purposes we can ignore it. However, different grist to liquor ratios will have an effect on mash pH, a thin mash will have a higher pH than a thick mash. This should be borne in mind if small adjustments to mash pH are required. Typical grist to liquor ratio can vary from about 1.5 litres per kilogram to about 3.5 litres per kilogram without much difference being experienced in extract or residual sweetness. Lagers sometimes employ grist to liquor ratios of up to 5 litres per kilogram. In general we aim for a figure somewhere in the middle of the range, being about 2 to 2.5 litres per kilogram, or about 1.6 pints of water per pound of grain in yesterspeak. This means that a typical bitter using about 4Kg of malt will require 8 to 10 litres of mash liquor.

Mash efficiency

For every kilogram of grain employed in the grist, we would expect to achieve a particular extract. For instance, pale malt has a typical laboratory extract of 297 degrees per kilogram litre. This means that, under laboratory conditions, the recovered wort from a small mash containing 1 kilogram of pale malt would have a maximum specific gravity of 1.297, or 1297 per litre. If the recovered volume of wort was five litres the original gravity of the wort would be 297/5 – about 1059. This assumes that we have good mashing efficiency. However, mashing efficiency is dependant upon the type of mash tun, the volume of grist employed, and the method of sparging used; therefore, in practice, the laboratory figures are never achieved. Many commercial breweries only achieve mash efficiencies of about 85%, and we should not expect any better. Typically we will achieve about 85% efficiency with ordinary strength ales, and, about 80% efficiency with strong ales. Extraction calculations are covered elsewhere in this book.

Maximum possible mashed extract

The strongest 100% mashed brew that we are able to produce is governed by the size of the equipment available to us. Home brewing equipment is based upon a brew length 5 gallons or 22.5 litres. All of the equipment available to us; brew bins, boilers and mash tun are based upon 22.5 litre batches, and at best might hold 25 litres. A mash tun based upon a fermenting bin could hold about 7.5 kg of malt along with the minimum quantity of about 2 litres per kilogramme of liquor. At 80% mashing efficiency we could expect a beer of about 1079 original gravity. However, at this concentration, sparging becomes difficult, and we end up with more than 25 litres of wort after we have sparged down to 1005. This means that, not only would a double boil be required, but prolonged boiling time would be necessary in order to reduce the volume back to 25 litres. In my experience the absolute maximum gravity that we can expect to extract, keep good sparging efficiency, and end up with a manageable volume of collected wort is about 1065, and that needs care. If we wish to brew stronger ales than this, then we will need to add sugars or syrups to our boil.

Another way of increasing maximum gravity is of course not to sparge. The brewers of yesteryear did not sparge their wort in quite the same way as we do now, sparging was not introduced until the early part of the nineteenth century. They mashed much larger quantities of malt per batch, twice or three times as much, and mashed the same batch up to three times; or at least, they thought that they were mashing three times. The first mashing made the strong old nectars of perhaps O.G. 1090 or 1100, the second mashing made the good quaffing ale of perhaps 1055, and the third mash made table beer (T beer) or small beer of about 1035 or 1040. Sometimes the first and second mashes were combined to brew a strong ale of O.G. around 1065 to 1075. However, the second and third mashes were not real mashes at all, merely rinses.

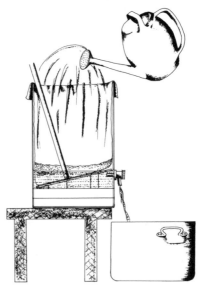

Sparging the grains

Strike heat

The starting temperature of the mash is usually around 66°C (called initial heat). However, the mixing of the cold grist with the liquor lowers the temperature of the liquor somewhat. In order to compensate for this temperature drop, the liquor is heated to a temperature a few degrees higher than initial heat prior to the grist being added, such that when the grist is added the temperature of the mash falls to the initial heat value (around 65°C). This higher temperature is known as strike heat and is usually about 72°C. The optimum value of strike heat is dependent upon the grist to liquor ratio and the temperature of the grist. It is best determined by experiment. If the strike heat is too high some of the conversion enzymes in the malt may be denatured, and yet if it is too low the temperature of the mash may fall too far below the desired initial heat and an inefficient mash may result.

Retorrefication

Obviously, the temperature difference between strike heat and initial heat is important. The closer strike heat is to initial heat the better. Anything that we are able to do to reduce this temperature difference is to our advantage. One technique for reducing the temperature difference is that of warming the grist prior to mashing, a technique known as retorrefication. Fortunately it is fairly easy for us to utilise this technique. All we need to do is to put our grist into a dry, 12.5 litre brewing bin with a tight close fitting lid, fit the lid and float it in our hot liquor tank as the mash liquor is being heated. Obviously, the temperature of our grist will be close to the temperature of our mash liquor, therefore the mash temperature will not drop (much) when the grist is added to the mash liquor. The only precautions that need to be taken are to ensure that the grist remains dry during retorrefication.

The mash

Prior to the mash the hot liquor tank is filled with treated brewing liquor and heated to a temperature of about 2°C or 3°C above strike heat. When this temperature has been attained, a quantity of liquor equivalent to about 2 litres per kilogram of grist is allowed to flow into the mash tun. The lid is fitted to the mash tun and a few minutes are allowed to elapse to enable the temperature of the liquor in the tun to stabilise. When a sufficient length of time has elapsed, a check on temperature is made to ensure that the temperature of the liquor is at strike heat about 78°C. Corrections to the temperature can be made by stirring in cupfuls of cold or boiling water as appropriate until the desired temperature has been attained.

When proper strike heat has been achieved, the grist can be added. The grist should be added as quickly as possible stirring frequently, but care should be taken to ensure that the grist is not added so fast that it is likely to cake into dry clumps. A gradual sprinkling motion is required, not a resounding splosh. When all of the grist has been introduced to the tun it should be thoroughly stirred to ensure that there are no dry pockets, and a check on temperature should be made to ensure that the temperature is at the desired initial heat. If it is not, it should be adjusted as quickly as possible by adding cupfuls of boiling or cold water, while stirring, until the temperature is correct. A note should be made of the original error in initial heat, and for future brews the strike heat should be adjusted accordingly to eliminate the need for further adjustments at this stage. The lid should be fitted to the mash tun and thermal insulation placed over the lid. It should then be left to stand for the appropriate time of around two hours. One should refrain from continually removing the lid of the tun and peering inside, otherwise too much heat may be lost in the process. A thermometer can be pushed through a hole in the lid of the tun to enable a check on temperature to be kept.

Adjustments to mash pH

Careful control of mash conditions will provide us with dependable, predictable, and repeatable results. It is very rare for a mash to fail completely because of incorrect mash conditions. The process is surprisingly tolerant and recovers well after corrective measures have been taken. Ensuring the mash temperature is correct is of primary importance during mashing; control of mash pH should assume secondary importance. Mash pH is controlled to a large extent by the water treatment prior to brewing, and correct water treatment should automatically ensure that the mash pH is correct.

The first time a particular beer is brewed it is desirable to ensure that the pH of the mash is at the chosen value. After the temperature corrections have been made to the mash, and it has been allowed to stand about 5 minutes, a sample of the wort should be drawn off in a test tube and cooled to room temperature under a tap. The pH of the sample should be measured and noted. The pH of the mash can be corrected by adding, directly to the mash, calcium carbonate if the pH is too low, or by adding calcium sulphate, (or lactic acid, or citric acid) if the pH is too high. The salts should be added, a teaspoonful at a time, stirring thoroughly until the desired pH is reached. A note of the quantity of added salts should be made, and for future brews the water should be treated appropriately. Calcium carbonate can be added to the mash to increase pH, but it is insoluble and should not be added directly to your water at the water treatment stage.

In general if the pH of the mash is too high there is either too much calcium bicarbonate in the water or insufficient calcium sulphate. If the pH is too low there is probably too much calcium sulphate in the water.

Once the correct water treatment has been determined for a particular type of beer, then it is fair to assume that the water treatment will be the same each time a similar beer is brewed and that our mash pH will automatically be correct.

Running off

When the appropriate mashing period has elapsed, it is obviously necessary to transfer the sweet wort from the mash tun into the boiler in readiness for the boiling stage of our beer production. Running off is accomplished by simply opening the tap in the mash tun and allowing the sweet wort to **gently** run into the boiler. The word gently must be emphasised because during the running off period, the grains in the mash tun settle down onto the false bottom and form a filter bed which serve to remove solid particles and debris from the wort. If the sweet wort is allowed to run off too fast, the filter action may be impaired, the grain may pack down and block causing a set mash, or debris may be drawn towards the tap and block that. The first runnings from the mash are likely to be turbid, and these should be returned to the mash tun until the sweet wort runs bright, after which time the sweet wort can be allowed to run into the boiler. As soon as the boiler's element is covered with wort, the heater should be turned on and the thermostat/simmerstat set to 77°C. This reduces the possibility of saccharification continuing in the collection vessel, but also it is desirable that the wort should not be allowed to cool before the boiling phase begins, which would favour the extraction of proteins and tannins and could cause off tastes and hazes to be produced in the finished beer. When the sweet wort has been run off, the goods in the mash tun (by now known as grains) still retain much of the sugary matter and this must be flushed out – or in brewerspeak, the grains must be sparged.

Sparging

Sparging consists of gently spraying the spent grains in the bottom of the mash tun with with hot water maintained at a temperature of about 77°C. The higher temperature helps to prevent the extraction of undesirable substances from the grains. Sparging must be performed gently, otherwise the filter bed of grain could crack and allow debris into the wort. Sparging is usually performed by heating the water in the hot liquor tank to a temperature of 77 – 80°C and spraying the water over the grains by means of a length of flexible pipe with a watering rose at one end and with the other end of the pipe connected to the boiler tap. A spray ring can be constructed from copper tubing if desired. If such refinements are unavailable, the simplest method is to simply pour jugfuls of hot water over the grains taking care to ensure that the bed does not break up.

The specific gravity of the spargings is monitored and sparging is halted when this falls to below about 1005. Over-sparging should be avoided because it favours the extraction of undesirable substances from the grains which cause off-tastes and hazes, apart from the risk of over diluting the wort. I must stress that sparging is a slow process; it must not be rushed. In commercial breweries, the run-off and sparging operation can take two hours or more. If you break up the mash bed and end up with a turbid wort; you may end up with a cloudy beer. Sometimes run-off and sparging are performed together. That is, the sparging is being performed at a rate which balances the outflow from the mash tun, thereby keeping the bed of grains floating.

Boiling

Once all of the wort has been collected the boiler is switched to full power, and we are ready for the boil. The boil is the subject of the next chapter.

Decoction mashing

The type of mash as described so far is the infusion mash and is typical of British brewing practice. Most of the rest of the world uses a different type of mashing system known as the decoction mash. The decoction mash features a low temperature protein rest period which enables an enzyme 'proteinase' to break down any proteins in the grist into amino acids and other low order nitrogenous products. A process known as proteolysis. The decoction mash was developed by the Germans in the latter half of the nineteenth century, apparently in order to cope with the poorer quality malt that was available to them, and to enable them to produce pale beers which matched the clarity of their English counterparts.

Traditionally the decoction mash is performed in an insulated mash tun in a similar method to the British infusion mash except that the initial mash temperature is maintained at 50°C for about an hour, this temperature being the optimum for proteolysis. After the mash has stood for an hour at 50°C, the temperature of the mash is increased to 65°C by removing 30% of the mash, boiling it in a separate vessel, and then returning it to the mash tun. 65°C being the optimum temperature for starch hydrolysis, or saccharification as in the infusion mash above. After the mash has stood for about an hour at 65°C, the temperature of the mash is then raised to 75°C by removing a further third of the mash, boiling it, and returning it to the mash tun. This higher temperature is the optimum for starch liquefaction which reduces wort viscosity and aids mash tun run off, it also deactivates the enzymes. As soon as the temperature has been raised to 75°C, the wort is run-off and the goods are sparged in the ordinary manner.

The decoction mash is quite easy for the home brewer to perform using an insulated mash tun. The low temperature protein rest period for proteolysis, is fairly temperature tolerant; a temperature of between 45°C and 55°C will give good results. In practice the liquor in the mash tun should be adjusted to a strike heat of about 60°C. The temperature of the overall mash will then drop to about 50°C when the grist is added. The decoction mash requires a greater liquor to grist ratio than is typical of the infusion mash, the mash being rather on the 'thin' side. About 3 litres of liquor per kilogram of grist being a typical figure, but any ratio between about 2 and 5 litres per kilogram will suffice. The temperature of the mash can be raised to 65°C by removing about 30% of the mash (wort and grain), boiling it in a saucepan, and then returning it to the mash tun and stirring it in. The saccharification temperature of 65°C is more critical than the proteolysis temperature, so particular care must be exercised when raising the mash temperature to ensure that the correct amount of mash is boiled to bring the main mash to the correct temperature without actually exceeding it. It is probably easier to boil several small amounts of the mash and gradually bring the main mash up to temperature in several stages. Emergency temperature corrections can be made by adding hot or cold water if necessary. The final part of the process, performed at a temperature of 75°C, is not critical, and is, in fact, not an essential part of the process. It serves to arrest sacharrification, and make the sweet wort less viscous, which aids run-off.

Temperature programming

A more modern equivalent to the decoction mash is known as a temperature programmed mash. It is exactly the same as the decoction mash except that the temperature is raised by means of a heater and not by boiling part of the mash. The term 'decoction' describes the action of boiling part of the mash, so this method can not properly be termed a decoction mash, although for most intents and purposes it is identical. The temperature programmed mash has one advantage over the traditional decoction; the action of boiling about one third of the mash to raise the overall mash temperature to 65°C destroys one third of the available enzymes necessary for saccharification. This may be fine for high nitrogen, poorly modified continental malts that are rich in enzymic activity, but the British low nitrogen, well modified malts are not particularly rich in enzymes, therefore the practice of destroying one third of the enzymes is considered undesirable. The temperature programmed mash gradually raises the tem-perature to the new level, thereby preserving the enzymes. The temperature programmed mash does find application in some British breweries, sometimes for lager production only, but often to produce English style beers when a large proportion of adjuncts are used in the grist makeup. The low temperature protein rest period can be used to degrade protein contained in the adjuncts, thereby producing a beer with less haze potential.

The temperature programmed mash is available to the home brewer. It is easier and more reliable than the traditional decoction mash. A one kilowatt kettle element fitted to an insulated mash tun is more than sufficient to raise the temperature of the mash to the new limits, a thermostat is not necessary or desirable, although a simmerstat type of controller can be fitted if desired. The temperature is raised to the new level by simply turning the heater on and carefully monitoring the temperature. For the first temperature step at least, the mash should be stirred frequently to even out the temperature gradient, great care should be taken ensure that hot spots are not developed which could destroy some of the enzymes. The temperature can be raised in stages by turning the heater on for short periods, if desired. Once the desired temperature has been reached the heater is switched off, the thermal insulation of the tun being responsible for maintaining the temperature. The second temperature step is not as critical, although care should be taken to avoid burning the grain.

The remainder of the mash is identical to the decoction mash. A thin mash is employed. The mash is started at a temperature of between 45°C and 55°C and maintained at this temperature for up to one hour for proteolysis to complete. The temperature is then raised to the desired mash temperature of around 65°C and maintained at this temperature for up to one and a half hours for the 'mash proper'. The temperature of the mash is then raised to a temperature of between 70°C and 75°C to complete starch liquefaction and assist run-off, the mash tun is then run off and sparged in the normal manner.

10 Boiling and cooling

A fierce fountain of wort, filled with the disrupted Hops, rises at the back of the Copper to the height of several feet, and the foaming liquid surges in a frothy mass till it nears the lip of the vessel. Then the Copper-men take great 'oars,' with blades of latticed wood, and beat the surface till it subsides.
(From 'A VISIT TO THE BASS BREWERY' 1902, Courtesy The Bass Museum.)

The boil is one of the most important stages in the brewing process, although it is the simplest to perform. The boil destroys any bacteria that may be present in the wort, destroys the enzymes which prevents further saccharification, drives off undesirable compounds in the wort, extracts the bittering substances from the hops, caramelises some of the sugars in the wort which provide colour and flavour. The boil also causes certain undesirable nitrogenous compounds to be driven off, and causes proteins to coagulate, thereby improving the stability of the finished beer.

A typical boiling period is from one to two hours. Generally, the longer the boil, the better is the stability of the finished beer. It is during the boil that the hops and any sugars or syrups called for in the recipe are added to our wort. The hops and sugars are added when the wort begins to boil, but sometimes about 25% of the hops are held back and added during the last fifteen minutes. This is done because some of the flavour and aroma giving substances derived from the hops are volatile and distill-off during the boil, although the preservative properties of the hops still remain. This last 25% of the hops are known as late hops and should be of the very best quality.

Another substance which is often added during the boil is **copper finings**, which serve to assist in the clarification of the wort during and after the boil. The most commonly used copper fining agent is **Irish moss**, sometimes called **carragheen**, but it is, in fact, a powdered, dried, seaweed or substances extracted from it. Colloids extracted from the Irish Moss during the boil combine with proteins and other solid particles in the wort, assisting them to settle out when the boil is completed. The colloids extracted from the moss are negatively charged, which attract positively charged particles (proteins), these then combine and settle out. Some residual extract from the moss will carry across to the finished beer and act as auxiliary finings.

Driving off undesirable substances

There are a number of substances derived from the malt, or produced during the mash which are present in small quantities in our sweet wort. If they are allowed to remain, these substances can cause off-tastes or hazes to be produced in our finished beer. Fortunately the most objectionable of these substances are volatile and are driven off during the boil, however, it is important that an extremely vigorous boil is developed, with plenty of mechanical action, in order to ensure complete volatilisation of these unwanted products. A mere simmer is insufficient. Most commercial breweries have a passive device fitted to their copper which behaves in much the same way as a coffee percolator. This keeps the wort in continuous circulation, thereby increasing the mechanical action and reducing the amount of energy required for the boil. Another advantage of the calandria, as the device is called, is that the circulating wort is brought into continuous contact with air, thereby facilitating some of the oxidisation processes that take place during the boil.

Coagulation of protein

One of the most important aspects of the boil is the coagulation and eventual precipitation of the proteins and other nitrogenous compounds in the wort. An excess of protein in the wort will give rise to hazes developing in the finished beer during storage. Protein hazes do not usually effect the flavour of the beer to any great extent, but they spoil the aesthetic appearance somewhat, usually resulting in the pint being rejected by the drinker. All real beer will contain some residual protein, because the only effective way of removing it completely is by chilling the beer to force a protein haze to be thrown, and then filtering it out. It is quite normal for a haze to be thrown when beer is chilled excessively, but it is nothing other than a protein haze and it will usually disappear again when the beer warms up to its proper temperature. However, the tendency for beer to haze at room temperature increases with its age, the temperature at which it is stored, and the quantity of these nitrogenous substances remaining in the beer. It is therefore desirable to ensure that the amount of protein and other nitrogenous compounds remaining in the beer is at a minimum. The boil has the effect of causing the protein to coagulate and form into globules or clumps, which will settle out when the wort is cooled. The longer the boil, the more protein will be precipitated, and the longer will be the shelf life of the finished beer.

Hot break

After the wort has been boiling for some time, the wort begins to haze as the proteins come out of solution. If the heat was turned off again the majority of these proteins would go back into solution or remain in suspension, however, after a prolonged boil of an hour or more, the molecular structure of the protein begins to break up and coagulate into a dark sticky substance. The colloidial nature of these small particles causes them to stick to each other and, from this point on, they rapidly grow in size until they are too large to remain in solution. Thus, when the heat is turned off they settle onto the bottom of the boiler. The point at which this all begins to happen is termed the **hot break**, and the protein matter which settles out is termed **trub** in brewerspeak.

Cold break

After the hot break has been achieved, and the trub allowed to settle out, the wort will 'drop bright' and become clear. However, as the wort is cooled it will go cloudy again and more protein matter will precipitate out of solution as trub. The faster the wort is cooled, the greater is the quantity of this protein matter which drops out of solution. This is termed the **cold break** in brewerspeak. Again the trub is allowed to settle out before the wort is transferred to the fermentation vessel.

Crash cooling

Force-cooling of the wort after boiling has several benefits. The most important of these is that the wort is exposed to airborne contamination for a shorter period of time and is cooled below the optimum temperature for bacterial growth fairly quickly. Another benefit is that rapid cooling forces much more potential haze forming protein to be precipitated out of solution. To force more trub to be precipitated out of solution we must not only cool quickly, say within an hour, but we must also cool to quite a low temperature. The lower the temperature, the more trub will be precipitated. An important point to bear in mind is that fast cooling our wort by the means of adding cold water will not cause trub to precipitate, in fact the opposite is true, the increased volume will encourage the protein to remain in solution. Fast cooling the wort with the intention of forcing further precipitation of protein must be performed with the wort in its concentrated, undiluted state.

Unfortunately, in the home brewing environment, we are usually unable to cool our wort fast enough to cause a significant amount of trub to drop out of solution; even if we could rapidly cool our wort, it is unlikely to cause a significant increase in the quality of our beer, particularly if we employed copper finings during the boil. In general, we do not require the long shelf life, or the same degree of haze stability that commercial breweries require. The main advantage, to us at least, of cooling our wort is to reduce the time it takes to complete our brew. It can take several hours for a wort to cool to pitching temperature by natural means, and during that time, the wort is dangerously vulnerable to bacterial infection.

The most common method of wort cooling employed by the home brewer is to transfer the wort from the copper into a fermenting bin and then to stand it in a bath of cold water. However, carrying hot liquids in a 'squidgy' plastic container is a hazardous business, particularly if one is lugging it upstairs to the bathroom. Another method is to submerge a coil of thin walled copper, or plastic tubing into the hot wort and to run cold tap water through the coil. A home made wort cooler is described in chapter 4.

Practical boiling

In the home brew situation the 'copper' or boiler can often serve as the collection vessel to collect the **sweet wort** during mash tun run-off and sparging. Ideally, the sweet wort should not be allowed to cool before the boiling operation begins. If the copper is being used as the collection vessel, then, as soon as sufficient wort has been collected to cover the heating element, the boiler should be turned on and set to maintain the temperature of the wort at about 77°C. However, as soon as all of the wort has been collected, the thermostat is set to maximum and the boil started.

As soon as the wort comes to the boil (**'copper up'** in brewerspeak) the first batch of hops should be added. Adding the hops will cause copious foaming and should be performed carefully. The next stage is to add any sugars that are called for in the recipe. The sugars should be added gradually to ensure that they go into solution properly without settling onto the element and possibly burning. Commercial invert sugar, which often comes in blocks, or glucose chips should be broken up into the smallest practical particle size in order to ensure rapid solubility, this can be performed by means of a hammer or rolling pin as appropriate.

Boiling period

The wort should be boiled vigorously for a minimum period of one hour, preferably two, or until hot break occurs. Weaker beers generally require a longer boil than strong beers, sometimes as long as two and a half hours. A vigorous or 'good rolling boil' is essential to allow volatile products to escape, and for the oxidation processes to occur. The violence of the boil is far more important than the boiling period. Prolonged boiling will drive off subtle flavour compounds, but under boiling will produce an unstable beer; it is all a matter of compromise. It is generally accepted that optimum boiling conditions are achieved when the wort evaporation loss is about 10% per hour. Do not put the lid on the boiler or you will end up covered in hops! The first half an hour of the boil must be attended and watched very carefully. Excessive foaming, after the addition of the hops, should be beaten back, or stirred in, with a metal frying pan spatula or similar implement. Resist the temptation to turn down the boil unless absolutely necessary to prevent spillage. Eventually the foaming will subside and the boil can resume at full throttle.

About fifteen minutes before the end of the boil the remainder of the hops and the Irish moss (if required) are added. The normal quantity of Irish moss added is 5 grams per 25 litre batch, but as most of us do not have weighing equipment of sufficient resolution to weigh such small amounts, one level teaspoonful is a good approximation. Care should be exercised not to over-do the Irish moss application because an excess can have the opposite effect from that desired and actually stabilise the protein in solution, rather than pull it out.

When the wort has been boiled for the desired length of time the boiler should be switched off and a period of time, about half an hour, allowed for the trub to coagulate or settle out. The trub can be seen as dark gummy particles of various sizes, either floating on the surface, or dropping out of suspension. When the trub has coagulated, or settled out of suspension, the tap on the boiler should be gently opened and the wort allowed to flow into a receiving vessel situated at a lower level. Care should be exercised to ensure that as much of the trub as possible is left behind in the boiler. The spent hops should settle onto the false bottom and act as a filter bed. The first runnings from the copper will often contain a certain amount of trub, and should be returned to the copper until the wort runs bright. If you boil your hops within a grain bag you will not have the benefit of a filter bed, but care should still be taken to ensure that as much of the trub as possible is left behind. Don't worry unduly if some of the trub is carried over to the fermentation vessel, much of it will settle out or be carried to the surface with the yeast.

I do not recommend the sparging of hops, this runs the risk of extracting trub and other undesirable substances from them. If you wish to sparge yours, do it sparingly.

Wort cooling

Once all of your wort has been collected it is time for the cooling stage of your beer production. As I mentioned earlier, forced cooling will cause a further precipitation of trub from the wort, but in the home brewing environment we are generally unable to cool our wort fast enough to cause a significant amount of trub to drop out of solution.

Several methods of wort cooling have already been mentioned. If you are cooling the wort with the intention of forcing further precipitation of trub, it is important to perform the cooling operation with the wort in its undiluted state, that is, before any top up water is added.

If you are cooling simply to quickly bring the wort to pitching temperature, it is still desirable to leave the wort in its undiluted state for the primary cooling stage, the higher temperature gradient will cause more efficient cooling. When the wort has cooled to between 40°C and 45°C, the top up water can be added to bring the wort to the desired original gravity, and the resultant wort should then be pretty close to pitching temperature. Further precipitation of trub may have occurred during cooling, you may leave this in the fermentation vessel, or rack the wort off into another vessel, just as the fancy takes you. It probably does not make much difference.

Wort aeration

It will be remembered from the discussion on yeast that the yeast requires dissolved oxygen in the wort for the first part of its life cycle. The action of boiling the wort drives off the dissolved oxygen present in the wort, thus some oxygen must be admitted back into the wort if healthy yeast growth is to occur. Air will admit into solution better after the wort has cooled. The simplest method of admitting air into solution is by allowing the wort to flow **slowly** from the tap on your receiving/cooling vessel, via a fairly lengthy airborne drop, into the fermenting vessel situated below. Alternatively, a length of tubing and a watering rose may be fitted to the tap, where the fine spray developed will admit copious amounts of air into solution.

11 The fermentation

'At first the surface of the wort becomes covered with a yellow cream, which thickens by degrees till it assumes the appearance of a dirty snowdrift. This next cracks in every direction, and the fragments assume the form of white cauliflower heads with yellow tips. The white stalks grow and swell till the whole head becomes a flat-topped mass of frothy foam, continually breaking away into ragged ciffs. Last of all the foam swells and rises into billows of silky bubbles, and side boards are put up around the squares to prevent them overflowing on to the floor'.
(from 'A VISIT TO THE BASS BREWERY' 1902, courtesy The Bass Museum)

Note:

The subject of yeast and fermentation go hand in hand. Much of the background theory regarding the fermentation process is contained in the chapter on yeast. This chapter is mostly concerned with the more practical aspects of fermentation.

Adjusting original gravity

When the wort has been collected in the fermentation vessel, and cool, it will be necessary to dilute it down to the desired original gravity by topping up the fermentation vessel with water until the desired gravity is reached. The higher the original gravity of the wort, the higher will be the strength and body of the finished beer. It should also be borne in mind that high strength is certainly not a pre-requisite of good beer. Any recipe can be adjusted to provide a stronger or weaker version of the same beer by either using more or less ingredients, or by topping up the fermentation vessel with more or less water as appropriate.

Dissolved oxygen

As discussed in the chapter on yeast, it is essential that the wort contains a certain amount of dissolved oxygen for the early stages of yeast growth. When the wort is cool, measures should be taken to ensure that an adequate supply of dissolved oxygen exists in the wort.

Some home-brewers authors stress the importance of keeping air out of contact with wort almost to the point of paranoia, with the result that the yeast finds itself with a deficiency of oxygen during its first formative hours. The reason for this paranoia is the fear of contamination with airborne bacteria, and there is a risk, but the risk is very small. The point is that we need to introduce air into solution at some point prior to pitching the yeast. However, once the yeast has established itself and reverted to anaerobic respiration, air should not be permitted to come into contact with the wort again. This is important, not only from the aspect of bacterial contamination, but also to ensure efficient alcoholic fermentation by the yeast, and to reduce the possibility of the beer degrading by various oxidisation processes during maturation and storage.

There are various methods of admitting oxygen into solution, probably the simplest is to slowly pour the wort from container to container a few times, taking care to ensure that the wort comes into maximum contact with air. A more efficient method is to open the tap on one vessel, and allow the wort to flow slowly, via an airborne drop, into another vessel below, or to spray the wort from one container to another via a watering rose connected to the tap of the first vessel. The wort should be cool before this operation is performed.

Pitching the yeast

Once the wort has cooled to about 20°C, it is safe to pitch the yeast. A yeast starter solution should be made up a few days before the main brew is started to ensure that a sufficiently large volume of actively fermenting yeast is used for pitching. The entire contents of the starter bottle should be emptied into the wort and stirred in. The greater the volume of yeast used for pitching the faster and surer will be fermentation. Commercial breweries use up to 25% of the yeast recovered from a previous brew to pitch the next. This not only reduces the **lag phase**, ie the time lag between pitching and the yeast begining efficient alcoholic fermentation, but due to the fact that it is only necessary for the yeast to multiply about fourfold during fermentation, it reduces the possibility of the yeast throwing a mutation half way through fermentation, which would possibly ruin the beer.

Fermentation progress

A good deal can be learned about how fermentation is progressing by observing the surface of the wort. A perfect description of the appearance of the yeast head during the various stages of fermentation is afforded by the contempory description of 1902 which I have used as a header to this chapter.

The yeast should begin to collect on the surface of the wort within a few hours of pitching, and the 'dirty snowdrift' stage should be reached eight to ten hours after pitching.

The first head of yeast carries up debris in the form of dark flocculum, and scum, it is normal practice to skim off the debris to prevent it tainting the beer, taking care to leave as much of the clean yeast as possible undisturbed.

About 20 hours after pitching, the 'cauliflower heads' or 'stalks' should be formed, followed about eight hours later by the 'ragged cliffs'. 36 hours after pitching the ragged appearance of the mass should be subsiding, and finally, within 48 hours the 'billows of silky foam' should be evident, although perhaps not quite as dramatic as the contemporary description suggests.

This final stage indicates that the yeast has fully adapted to anaerobic respiration, yeast growth has diminished to a minimum, and the yeast is now is working flat out producing alcohol. The foaming is caused by the copius amount of CO_2 thus produced. If the dropping system of fermentation is being employed, it is at this stage that the fermenting wort is transfered or 'dropped' into the secondary vessel.

The above description is representative only, the actual appearance and the timing of the various stages is very dependent upon wort composition, original gravity, and fermentation temperature. It is important with a genuine top working brewer's yeast, that a thick fluffy head of yeast be formed on the surface of the wort, and I mean a thick fluffy head, two inches thick or more! If this is not achieved there is something wrong with either your yeast or your brewing technique.

It should be borne in mind that most beer kits use hop extracts as their source of bitterness, and that some strains of yeast will not perform well if the sole source of hop products is in the form of extracts. No one knows for sure why this should be so, but it is undoubtably the result of hundreds of years of training our yeast to like hopped beer. The only real solution, if you feel that you are suffering from poor yeast performance for this reason, is to use whole hops for part of your bitterness.

During the course of fermentation, the specific gravity of the wort will progressively fall as the sugars in the wort are converted to alcohol and carbon dioxide. The specific gravity of the wort should be frequently measured to ensure that fermentation is proceeding in a satisfactory manner.

The specific gravity at which fermentation is complete is called **final gravity**, and this varies depending upon the beer being made. Typically, a bitter with an original gravity of 1040 will ferment down to a final gravity of between about 1008 to 1010. A beer which has a large proportion of sugar in its makeup will ferment to a lower final gravity than will a 100% malt beer. Final gravity has been reached when the specific gravity of the beer remains more or less static for a period of twenty four hours.

Very often a beer will deliberately be barrelled or bottled before the beer has fermented down to final gravity in order to eliminate the need to add priming sugars. The specific gravity at which this is done is known as **racking gravity** and is usually 2 to 3 points above final gravity. This is covered in more detail in the chapter on finishing.

It is not necessary or desirable to fit the lid to the fermentation bin during the early stages of fermentation, it is important that the fermentation be allowed to breathe, so to speak. During the latter stages of fermentation, when activity is subsiding, a lid can be fitted if desired.

Fermentation Temperature

The temperature at which fermentation is conducted has a great effect upon the flavour of the finished beer. The correct fermentation temperature is of the utmost importance if consistent flavour and quality are desired. Unfortunately, the control of fermentation temperature within safe limits is one of the most difficult problems facing the home brewer. If the temperature is too high, a racing fermentation and astringent off-flavours may result, whereas if the temperature is too low, poor yeast performance may occur, which usually shows itself by the yeast losing its buoyancy and sinking into the wort, giving the appearance of reverting to bottom working. In my experience the ideal temperature is the minimum temperature at which good yeast performance is achieved. This varies between different types of yeast and wort composition, but is usually around 18°C. The maximum range of temperature recommended for top working brewer's yeast is between the limits of 15°C to 22°C. This sounds easy, but it is surprisingly difficult, particularly when one considers that fermentation takes about four days to complete, and for most of this time the majority of us should be out 'earning our crust', prohibiting us from giving the fermentation our total and undivided attention.

It should be borne in mind that the yeast provides many by-products other than ethanol and carbon dioxide. These have been mentioned elsewhere, but can be thought of as 'flavour compounds'. These flavour compounds have an important bearing on the final outcome of the finished beer, but are most apparent when fermentation is conducted at a high temperature and least apparent when fermentation is conducted at a low temperature. It therefore follows that a beer which has been brewed at a very low temperature may be somewhat bland in flavour, whereas a beer that has been brewed at a high temperature may have flavour compounds that are somewhat overpowering or even unpleasant. Obviously a sensible balance must be achieved.

Energy, in the form of heat, is evolved in the course of fermentation, which would normally cause the temperature of the wort to gradually rise. However, in our home brewing environment the ratio of volume of wort to the surface area of our vessel is such that this temperature rise is not usually apparent. We can take advantage of this evolved heat to increase the temperature of fermentation, if desired, by lagging our vessel with Rockwool or fibreglass insulation as described for the mash tun in the equipment chapter. When the temperature has risen to its maximum we can cool the wort by removing the lagging, and/or moving the vessel to a cooler place as appropriate.

A number of traditional commercial breweries pitch their yeast when the wort has cooled to about 16°C, and allow the temperature of the wort to rise naturally to a maximum of about 22°C about half way through fermentation, at which point they turn on the cooling water and gradually pull the temperature down such that it is back to 16°C at the end of fermentation.

We normally control the temperature of fermentation by moving our fermentation vessel to a warmer or colder location as appropriate. Unfortunately it is very much easier to raise the temperature of fermentation than it is to lower it, raising the temperature can be accomplished by means of a brewers immersion heater, by standing the vessel on a winemakers heated mat, or by lagging the vessel if the yeast is still actively fermenting. In the winter there is always somewhere in the house warm enough for satisfactory fermentation. Lowering the temperature, particularly in warm weather, is an entirely different matter. Ideally one should not brew in the summer months, because 'summer brewed ale doth not keep' (Brakspear). Cooling can be accomplished by standing the vessel in a bath of cold water, or by means of an **attemperator**, a coil of copper or plastic piping submerged in the wort with cold water flowing through it. The flow can be adjusted to maintain the desired temperature.

Fermentation pH

The acidity of the wort (pH) also has an important bearing on yeast activity. However, if we are brewing using established techniques, the pH of the wort should automatically be correct, and we should not need to concern ourselves with the subject any further. If one is consistantly having difficulties with yeast perfomance, then it is worth checking wort pH at the beginning of fermentation to see that things are okay, but otherwise we can safely forget it. The ideal **starting** acidity for fermentation is around pH 5.0, but anything around pH 5.3 is satisfactory. Most brewing methods, including brewing from malt extract, provide a starting pH of around 5.3. Starting pH is stressed because the pH of the wort falls very quickly during the course of fermentation, reaching a lower level of about pH 4 towards the end. The pH of the wort can be adjusted, if desired, by adding lactic acid or citric acid to lower it, or by adding calcium bicarbonate, magnesium sulphate, or ammonium phosphate to raise it. But again, I stress, that it should not be necessary.

The dropping system

It is usual with home brewing to ferment out completely in a single fermentation vessel, and very good beer can be brewed in this manner. However, it was the practice with the best breweries of old to utilise the dropping system, whereby about halfway through fermentation, the fermenting wort was carefully 'dropped' into another vessel, leaving much of the surplus yeast, trub, and other debris behind. This practice has now largely disappeared due to the poor vessel utilisation which it affords.

The dropping system merely entails transferring the wort to a secondary fermentation vessel about half way through fermentation, leaving as much as possible of the surplus yeast behind. The exact point at which the wort is transferred is dependant upon the type of beer being brewed, but should be done just after the yeast has fully adapted to anaerobic respiration, which corresponds with the 'billows of silky bubbles' stage of fermentation mentioned above. This is typically 48 hours after pitching, but it is not particularly critical.

The wort should be carefully transferred, leaving as much of the yeast as possible behind, by means of a syphon tube or by means of a length of tubing connected to the tap of the primary vessel. The outlet end of the tubing should be submerged in the wort being transferred to the secondary vessel to ensure that a minimum of air goes into solution.

Skimming yeast

Many early books (and some recent ones) on the subject of home brewing advocated the practice of regularly removing surplus yeast from the surface of the wort, and it has now become fairly common practice in home brewing circle to do so. The argument being that dead yeast cells will fall into the beer and taint it. One very recent home brewing book expends several paragraphs giving precise instructions for first head removal, second head removal, and third head removal! When one considers the considerable amount of effort that we expend at every stage of beer production to ensure that conditions are correct for the optimum working of our yeast, such that we get a thick rocky head on the surface of our wort, it is rather amusing to learn that as soon as the thick yeast head is formed, many people immediately skim it off again!

It is, in fact, not necessary or desirable to be continually skimming surplus yeast from the surface of the wort. We should be using a top working brewer's yeast, and while it is sitting on top, it is actually doing its job properly! The argument for dead yeast cells tainting the beer does not really stand up to criticism. The dead yeast cells, mutant strains, flocculum, trub, and other matter are more likely to be sitting it out on the **bottom** of the fermentation vessel, therefore, removing healthy yeast from the **top** is not likely to help much. In any case, unless you tend to produce beers which are highly toxic, one hopes that you will not have too many dead yeast cells to worry about!

Of course, any muck that is brought up with the initial crop of yeast should be skimmed off, and anything else that looks undesirable should be removed. You will also be forced to do some skimming if the yeast is in danger of overflowing onto the floor, but, apart from this, you can safely leave the yeast to its own devices until either you drop the beer into a secondary vessel, or until it is approaching the end of fermentation.

The yeast should be skimmed when the wort has fermented to within a few points of final gravity, say at about 1013 for a 1045 O.G. bitter. Remove as much of the yeast as possible, using a flour sieve or similar implement, and then fit the lid and airlock to the bin until racking gravity or final gravity has been reached.

Rousing

Sometimes a yeast will find it difficult to ferment a particular beer and fermentation will unaccountably stop, or at least slow down considerably. Some strains of yeast flocculate early and spend all of their time sitting on top of the wort, when they should be in suspension doing some work. These yeasts must be frequently roused by stirring it back into suspension.

Rousing normally refers to the practice of stirring the head of yeast into the beer to stimulate the yeast back into action, but sometimes the yeast is roused by re-oxygenating the wort.

Another problem is a condition that winemakers refer to as a stuck fermentation, which is caused by there being too much glucose present for the yeast to cope with. Not only does the yeast find it difficult to move around and operate in a very thick, gooey, viscous medium, but also, high concentrations of glucose (or cane sugar) retard osmosis and cause the yeast to go into a form of suspended animation. Sometimes rousing will cure the problem, but very often it is necessary to re-oxygenate the wort to stimulate the yeast into briskness. Once the specific gravity drops below a certain level the problem often goes away.

The last cause is a matter of yeast training. Most yeasts will refuse to operate efficiently if they are suddenly asked to ferment a wort that is much higher in original gravity than the worts in which it is accustomed to working. A yeast that has spent the last few generations of its life fermenting a 1035 beer may object if it is suddenly asked to ferment a 1065 beer. This is the problem that we are most likely to encounter, and rousing usually cures the problem. If the yeast is frequently asked to ferment a 1065 beer it will often adapt itself, and subsequently ferment the wort without problems.

Once the specifc gravity of the ferment has fallen to racking gravity of final gravity, we are ready for the finishing stage of our beer production. The subject of the next chapter.

12 Finishing

'Blessing of your heart, you brew good beer'
(Shakespeare)

Introduction to this chapter

The term 'finishing' in this context applies to any operation which is performed after fermentation. Barrelling, bottling, priming, fining, dry hopping, and maturing, are all operations which I have termed finishing.

Transferring beer from vessel to vessel

Transferring the beer from one container to another should be performed with care. Aeration of the beer should be avoided at all cost. The secondary vessel and the transfer tubing should be clean and sterile. Care should be exercised to ensure that a minimum of air comes into contact with the beer and that any sediment is left behind in the primary vessel. The beer can be transferred by either syphoning using a suitable syphon tube or by fitting a length of tubing to the tap of the primary vessel. In either case the tube should be long enough to reach to the bottom of the secondary vessel, such that the end of the tube is submerged under the beer being transferred to minimise air being absorbed into solution.

Dry hopping

Dry hopping is the name given to the practice of adding a few hop cones to the barrel at the time of barrelling the beer. This is done to improve the hoppy aroma of those beers that are expected to have a hoppy aroma, normally best bitters and pale ales. Dry hopping does not increase the bitterness of beers. About 10 grams of the finest aroma type hops, either Goldings or Fuggles, per 25 litre batch of beer, is usually employed for this purpose. However, I have my doubts about the practice of putting raw hop cones into finished beer, despite the fact that it has been practiced for centuries. Not only does it take some time for the benefit of dry hopping to be felt in the beer, which should not be a problem to home brewers, but I feel that it rapidly goes past its best and eventually a harsh astringent flavour is extracted from the hops which spoils the beer. This is probably due to tannin and other undesirables being extracted from the bracts and stalks.

A preferable method is to stir the hops into the copper wort immediately after the boil, just after the heat has been switched off, and leave for half an hour or so before draining the copper. This way there is no debris remaining to taint the beer with age.

Priming

Priming is the technique of putting a small quantity of either sugar, wort, or malt extract into the barrel or bottles in order to provide secondary conditioning gas. The residual yeast contained in the beer ferment these additional materials to provide the carbon dioxide sparkle and secondary condition.

Generally speaking, a properly formulated and properly brewed beer should not need priming. There should be sufficient residual sugars remaining in the beer at the time of barrelling to provide secondary fermentation and condition. Priming should only be used if the beer has been accidentally allowed to go very flat, or if we wish to sweeten a beer, such as a stout, or if experience indicates that sufficient condition is not achieved without priming.

If priming is deemed necessary, white cane sugar can be added directly to the barrels or bottles, in which case 5 grams per litre is a typical quantity to use. This equates to about 1/2 a teaspoonful per pint bottle or 125 grams per 25 litre batch in the barrel. It is better to add these sugars as a syrup, which not only ensures that the sugar is completely sterile, but ensures that the sugar goes into solution easily, and also eliminates the possibility of grains of sugar becoming trapped under the crown closures when bottling, which would damage the gas tight seal. To make a suitable syrup; place 150 grams of sugar into a domestic 300 ml tea/coffee mug (not cup) and top up the mug with boiling water from the kettle, stirring continuously to ensure that the sugar is dissolved. When the sugar has dissolved, cover the mug with a saucer and leave to cool. A suitable priming rate for the resultant syrup is 1 level teaspoonful per pint bottle, or tip the whole contents of the mug into the barrel.

White sugar is 100% fermentable and its use as a priming sugar can have the effect of drying the flavour of the beer if used to excess. This can be overcome by priming with malt extract, barley syrup, or corn syrup where the residual dextrins will maintain the sweetness balance. A similar syrup to the above can be made by warming 200 grams of malt extract, barley syrup, or corn syrup in a saucepan, transferring it to the 300 ml coffee mug, topping up the mug with boiling water as before, stirring to ensure that it goes into solution. The priming rate is the same as with the cane sugar syrup.

The addition of the new artificial sweeteners such as Aspartame, NutraSweet, or Canderel, to the priming sugars can serve to sweeten stouts and other beers should it be necessary. The quantity employed is again a matter of taste. Two teaspoonsful per 25 litre batch is a good starting point for a sweet stout. Do not use Saccharin, it supplies a funny taste. Remember that these artificial sweeteners are non fermentable and will not provide condition. They should be used in conjunction with a fermentable sugar, such as cane sugar or malt extract, if you need to promote condition. An old text states that beet sugar is unsuitable for priming: '*Beet sugar may entail defective cask fermentation, with faulty fining, and probably ropiness*'.

Krausening

Krausening is the term applied to priming the beer with actively fermenting wort, and was begun in Germany because the sterile filtering process, which was invariably used to clarify their beer, also removed the yeast. A small quantity of yeast, and some additional fermentable matter needed to be introduced into the beer to give it secondary condition. The same technique was often practised in England, as an acceleration technique for bringing blended old stouts, which were flat but otherwise wholesome, into condition. A technique known as 'Gyle priming' or 'Gyle worting'. At one time bottled stouts were a mixture of several matured stouts of different ages which were blended and then gyle worted before bottling (Bottled Guinness still is, I believe). The gyle wort was taken from a fermenting vessel towards the end of fermentation.

In the home brewing field we should not need to gyle prime or krausen or beers because we do not filter, we should have sufficient active yeast cells in suspension to achieve secondary condition.

Fining

For the last several hundred years at least, it has been the common practice of commercial breweries to aid the final clearing of beers by the addition of colloidial or alginate type substances. A process known as **fining**. Strictly speaking, in the home brewing environment, it should not be necessary to fine our beers unless it is particularly troublesome. A well balanced beer, fermented with a good strain of genuine top working brewer's yeast, will clear down unaided. Commercial breweries fine their beers because the beers get shaken during transportation to the pub, and secondary clearing could take many days, if they cleared at all. Fining does improve the shelf life of a beer, and greatly reduces the risk of a protein haze being thrown, which is important to a brewery, but in the home brewing environment the beer is usually drunk before these problems have a chance to show themselves. However, fining may sometimes be necessary.

Gelatine
Gelatine is usually manufactured from the hooves of cattle, and is the earliest of all fining agents. It is the most convenient and the most popular form of finings for the home brewer, although it is not often used by British commercial

breweries. Gelatine is a useful fining agent because it is sticky; that is, its fining power is achieved by the unwanted particles sticking to it on its way down through the beer. This means that it will clear almost any type of unwanted particle out of the beer, unlike other fining agents which will only clear particles holding a particular ionic charge.

Bear in mind that gelatine does not have a very powerful secondary fining effect, so if you anticipate lugging your beer from Bognor to Bangor, fine your beer at Bangor not Bognor. Fining is usually performed after a suitable maturation period or a few days before the beer is likely to be drunk. Davis Gelatine is the tool usually employed by home brewers, one 12 gram sachet dissolved in a cup full of hot water is sufficient for a 25 litre batch of beer. When the cup of finings is cool, the barrel is carefully opened, a couple of pints of beer drawn off in a jug, the cup full of dissolved gelatine added to the jug and stirred in, and the jug of beer carefully returned to the barrel. If the beer is going to be drunk in a short period of time, primings may need to added at the same time.

Isinglass

Isinglass is manufactured from the swim bladder of the South African sturgeon fish by acid treatment. Isinglass is the fining agent most commonly used by British breweries, and is in fact superior to gelatine in both its clearing power, and in its ability to continually re-fine the beer if it gets shaken. Isinglass has a positive ionic charge and it clears the beer by attracting negatively charged particles, such as yeast, rather like a magnet. As you know, like-poles repel, this repulsion effect causes the isinglass particles to space themselves out evenly through the beer and fall down through it, attracting negatively charged particles on the way, rather like a web. If too much isinglass is used, the charge effect can cause the isinglass to be balanced in suspension, causing the opposite effect to that desired, although the treatment must be grossly overdone for this to happen. Another problem with isinglass is that the optimum quantity for maximum fining power is a matter of experiment, and thus it must be used with caution.

Isinglass is not popular among home brewers, partly because gelatine does an adequate job cheaply, and without too many problems, and partly because of the lack of stability of isinglass. In its liquid state isinglass deteriorates very rapidly at ambient temperatures, becoming ineffective as a result. It must be stored below 20°C, preferably in a refrigerator. Make sure your home brew shop actually stores the isinglass in a refrigerator, otherwise don't buy it. The earliest mention of the use of isinglass for clearing beer was in 'Every Man His Own Gauger' published in the year 1695! This is incredible when one considers its origins, its manufacturing process, and the fact that they did not have refrigerators in those days!

Isinglass finings are also available in dry form, and in this form the shelf life of the powder is two years. However, dry finings are difficult to prepare, and do not find favour in home brewing. Dry finings should be mixed with the appropriate quantity of cold water in a high speed food mixer for as long a period as possible, preferably one hour. The finings should then be allowed to stand for twelve hours before use. Of course, once mixed, the finings will have the same stability problems as the liquid form, but, nevertheless, the prepared finings will keep for many weeks in a refrigerator.

Dry Isinglass is usually added to beer at the rate of about 50 milligrams per litre of beer to be fined, after first preparing it as above, and then mixing it with a quantity of beer equivalent to about 1% − 2% of the total volume to be treated.

Liquid finings, in their ready to use state, come in various concentrations so the instructions should be read carefully. Again the appropriate quantity of finings should be mixed with some beer (about half a pint for a 5 gallon batch) before being added to the main bulk of the beer.

The finings should not be added before beer has had a short maturation period, a minimum of a week, but are usually added a few days before drinking. Isinglass finings should not be added to beer if its temperature is above 18°C., nor should the temperature of fined beer be allowed to rise above about 20°C for any length of time, ideally the temperature of the beer should be lowered to below 13°C. before the finings are added.

Auxiliary finings

Auxiliary finings are a special form of finings which remove positively charged particles from our beer − namely proteins and other nitrogenous matter. They behave in the same way as isinglass finings but have the opposite ionic charge. Yeast in suspension is negatively charged and isinglass, being positively charged, is used to remove this. However, haze forming proteins are positively charged and auxiliary finings, being negatively charged, are used to remove these. Copper finings are a form of auxiliary finings and this should be sufficient to guard against a protein haze in our home brew environment. Adding auxiliary finings at any other stage should only be necessary, home brew or commercially, if an accident has occurred in brewing.

Auxilliary finings are commonly made from alginates, and are negatively charged. They should only be used if your beer is not clearing properly with isinglass treatment, but it should be obvious that auxiliary finings are not a substitute for isinglass.

It should not be necessary to add auxiliary finings if Irish moss is used during the boiling phase, because enough residual extract from the moss should be left in the beer to act as auxiliary finings. Care must be taken in the use of auxiliary finings because an excess will stabilise and remain in suspension. Auxiliary finings can be used to neutralise an excess of isinglass finings and vica versa. Dry auxiliary finings are available from specialist suppliers and mix readily in cold water, It is however relatively easy to make your own. Thus:

Put 300 ml of water into a small saucepan and bring to the boil, add two teaspoons full of Irish moss (caragheen), a pinch of magnesium sulphate, and a pinch of calcium sulphate. Boil gently for ten minutes. Allow to cool. If the final volume is less than 200 ml, bring it back up to this figure by adding water. If the solution is to be stored as a stock solution, a pinch of sodium met. and a pinch of citric acid will help to stabilise it against bacterial infection, store it in a refrigerator.

The correct rate of usage must be found by experiment. If Irish moss was used during the boiling phase of your beer production then 25 mL of the solution per 25 litre batch is a good starting point. If Irish moss was not used during the boiling phase then 50 ml is a good starting point. Mix the finings with about half a pint of beer before adding it to the main batch.

It is best to add auxiliary finings at the racking stage of beer production, but they can be added at stage thought necessary. Auxiliary finings should not be added at the same time as isinglass, otherwise they will neutralise each other and nothing will happen. A period of about three days should be allowed between the addition of auxiliary finings and isinglass and vice versa.

It should not be necessary for the home brewer to use auxiliary finings, and I do not recommend the use of auxiliary finings as a matter of course, except in the form of copper finings.

Bacterial control and Redox treatments

Most commercial breweries usually add some other ingredients to the beer at the time of fining in order to improve the shelf life of the beer. The most common ingredient for this purpose is sulphur dioxide, which can be added in the form of sodium metabisulphite. Sulphur dioxide is not only a fairly powerful antibacterial compound to which our yeast has a very high tolerance, but by a complicated chain of events, sulphur dioxide also absorbs dissolved oxygen in the beer to the further detriment of any aerobic organisms which may be present. A typical concentration would be about 50 ppm of sulphur dioxide. This is achieved by adding 3.5 ml of 10% stock sodium metabisulphite solution or one campden tablet per 4.5 litres of beer.

Redox treatments are treatments which remove dissolved oxygen from the beer, and are performed by the means of adding antioxidants. Removing dissolved oxygen not only prevents aerobic bacteria from establishing themselves, but many other degradation aspects of beer during storage are the result of oxidisation processes, removing dissolved oxygen also retards these. Brewer's yeast being anaerobic is unaffected by redox treatments. It is true that redox treatments are not likely to harm anaerobic bacteria, but most spoilage organisms which affect beer are aerobic, apart from which anaerobic organisms are unable to multiply anywhere near as fast as aerobic organisms. Sulphur dioxide is a fairly good antioxidant as well as being antiseptic. Absorbic acid is a much more powerful antioxidant but it has no antiseptic properties. Absorbic acid is nothing other than vitamin C, and can be used in conjunction with sulphur dioxide in the treatment of beer. Concentrations of 20 to 150 milligrams of absorbic acid per litre of beer is employed. Absorbic acid is available from your local home brew shop in convenient 100 milligram tablets. Fifteen of these, crushed and then added to a twenty five litre batch of beer is usually sufficient. Alternatively, if supplied in powder form, 1.5g or a level teaspoonful per 25 litre batch is the dose.

Maturing

A maturation period is always necessary after barrelling or bottling to enable the beer to come into condition. During the maturation period the full flavour of the beer is developed. A number of undesirable, harsh tasting substances are broken down into more mellow substances and various more volatile substances come out of solution and are given off to the atmosphere when the barrel is vented.

Stronger beers require more maturation time than do the weaker beers. As a rule of thumb, for barrelled beers, the original gravity of the beer in degrees, divided by two, will give a typical maturation period in days. A 1040 bitter requires $40/2 = 20$ days maturation whereas a 1060 bitter will require 30 days. All beers will benefit from a longer period of maturation, and most beers can be drunk in a much shorter time. All bottled beers should be first matured in barrel, and then a minimum of a month in bottle.

Barrelling

There are not any special precautions that need to be taken when barrelling, except to ensure that a minimum of air comes into contact with the beer. This can be achieved by filling the barrel by means of a long tube which reaches to the bottom of the barrel, always keeping the end of the tube submerged. Unless one is going to pressurise one's beer with a carbon dioxide injector, it is not necessary to use the expensive pressure barrels or spheres, because the cheaper form of barrel is perfectly adequate.

Bottling

All beer to be bottled should be matured in the barrel first. The home brew practice of bottling beer straight from the fermentation vessel is not to be recommended because maturation requires some undesirable substances to be driven off. These substances are given off to the atmosphere when the barrel is vented a few days prior to drinking (or bottling), obviously, this can not happen in a sealed bottle. According to an old text: '*Beers intended for bottling should be rolled daily for a week or fortnight from the time of racking to priming and stillaging, following which it should stand on stillage for six to eight days during which period condition is gradually released by shive peg.*' I have never gone to quite those lengths, but it does go some way to show that bottling beer does require some care and attention.

In general, the beer should be matured in barrel for a week or a fortnight, longer for very strong beers, and then stillaged in a cool place in a suitable position for bottling. Before bottling, vent the barrel by releasing the air tight cap or by fitting a spare cap modified to take an airlock. The action of venting the barrel should cause some fermentation to resume. If the beer does not become active, it will be necessary to prime the beer. Keep a careful check on the activity of the beer. As soon as the beer is bright and sparkling, and in a quiet state, not fermenting, it is in the proper condition to be bottled.

Bottles should be filled by means of a long tube that reaches to the bottom of the bottle to minimise admitting air into solution. They should be filled to about an inch from the top. Only use bottles that are designed to hold beer and are therefore able to withstand the pressure generated by secondary fermentation. If priming sugars are necessary, they can be added directly to the bottle, but it is easier to add the sugar as a syrup to the beer a day or so prior to bottling. A couple of pints of beer should be drawn off, mixed with the previously prepared syrup and then returned to the barrel. A day or so should be allowed to elapse to allow the primings to distribute within the beer. If granulated sugar is being added directly to the bottles, it is best to add it via a funnel to eliminate the possibility of grains sticking to the lip of the bottle, which would prevent a gas tight seal when the closure is fitted. Bottled beer will take a month to six weeks to come into proper condition. 13°C is the optimum storage temperature for bottled beers.

Warm and cold conditioning

Warm and cold conditioning is an old conditioning technique which consists of a preliminary conditioning phase by standing the beer in a warm place (16°C to 20°C) for about a third of its maturation period, followed by moving the beer to a cold place (2°C to 8°C) for the remainder of its maturation period. Warm and cold conditioning is particularly applicable to bottled beers. Warm and cold conditioning can be employed by the home brewer by standing the beer in a warm room for about a week, taking care to ensure that the temperature of the beer does not exceed 20°C, followed by standing the beer in the coldest place you can find, such as the garage, for the remainder of its maturation period. If isinglass finings are used, these should be added during the cold phase, after the beer temperature has dropped to its lowest level.

A typical finishing procedure

During fermentation the specific gravity of the fermenting beer should be regularly monitored, and when it has reached racking gravity, which is two or three degrees above final gravity, the beer should be transferred to a racking vessel, taking care not to aerate the beer, and to leave as much sediment behind as is possible. A close fitting lid and airlock should be fitted to the vessel. The vessel should be moved to the coldest place that can be found and left for a minimum of about 24 hours. This will encourage surplus yeast to settle out. The beer can be stood in this condition for as long as desired.

After a suitable standing period, carefully transfer the green beer to the barrel, using a pipe which reaches to the bottom of the barrel, taking care not to admit air into solution, and taking care to leave any sediment behind in the racking vessel. Dry hops, redox treatments, auxiliary finings, and priming sugars can be added at this stage if desired, but do not add isinglass or gelatine finings. The beer should then be left to mature for the appropriate time.

If the beer is going to be fined, the finings should be added after a suitable maturation period has elapsed, anything from a couple of weeks to a month depending upon beer. To add the finings, the beer should be cooled as much as possible, the barrel opened, the finings added, and the barrel re-sealed. If the beer is going to be drunk within a very short period, it may be necessary to add some primings at the same time.

13 Cleanliness and sterilisation

'Gordon came back balancing two pint glasses of dark common ale. They were thick cheap glasses, thick as jam jars almost, and dim and greasy. A thin yellow froth was subsiding on the beer. The air was thick with gunpowdery tobacco-smoke. Ravelston caught sight of a well filled spittoon near the bar and averted his eyes. It crossed his mind that his beer had been sucked up from some beetle-ridden cellar through yards of slimy tube, and that the glasses had never been washed in their lives, only rinsed in beery water.........'
(From 'Keep The Aspidistra Flying' George Orwell, Penguin edition 1978)

The importance of complete cleanliness and proper sterilisation should go without saying. Wort is a perfect culture medium, full of nutrients and trace elements, ideal for the growth of moulds, bacteria, and other nasties such as wild yeasts. The finished beer is also capable of supporting certain types of bacteria, little 'animicules' which can spoil the beer during storage. Cleaning and sterilisation is a very important part of home brewing. It is important that all brewing items are cleaned immediately after use, and sterilised again immediately before the next time they are used. Not only should the fermenting bins, barrels, and bottles be sterilised, but also every other item that comes into contact with the beer. Do not forget lids, paddles, spoons, syphon tubes, thermometers, hydrometers, and the taps fitted to barrels and fermenting vessels.

Household bleach

Household bleach is a good and cheap cleaning and sterilisation agent. Apart from excellent cleaning properties, it also releases chlorine, which kills all known bugs. It is also excellent for cleaning heavily contaminated articles, such as badly contaminated beer bottles or barrels. A 5% solution of household bleach, that is one volume of bleach made up to twenty volumes by adding nineteen volumes of water, is a typical concentration for cleaning purposes. Very much lower concentrations can be employed for sterilisation duties. The articles to be cleaned should be immersed in the solution for about twenty minutes, brushed, and then very thoroughly rinsed afterwards.

Bleach requires very thorough rinsing to remove all traces of chlorine which would otherwise taste in the finished beer. After rinsing two or three times. It is important that glassware is not left in contact with the bleach solution for extended periods of time because the bleach will attack the glass and cause a frosted effect.

Sodium carbonate

Sodium carbonate is common washing soda, and is a much under-rated cleaning and degreasing agent. Do you remember those little blue boxes of ICI washing soda? It used to be used for just about everything! Well it is still available. It will dissolve hardened beer and yeast residues in the bottom of bottles. It is particularly valuable for washing glassware, where it leaves the items completely free of grease and gives them a pristine sparkle. It will also remove detergent residues from glassware which could cause poor head retention. For glass washing duties, one or two tablespoonsful in a bowl of hot washing up water is sufficient. For heavy duty cleaning much higher concentrations can be safely employed. Washing soda is most effective when used with hot water. It attacks aluminium, **DO NOT** use it on aluminium items.

Sodium hypochlorite

Sodium hypochlorite is a chlorine releasing agent and is, therefore, a powerful steriliser. Many commercial sterilising agents are based on sodium hypochlorite. Although it is a very effective sterilising agent, it is not a cleaning agent. Proprietary multi-purpose cleaning agents often use sodium hypochlorite in conjunction with Sodium metasilicate, or sometimes caustic soda. Sodium hypochlorite is available from many home brew shops, and should be used as directed.

Caustic soda

Sodium hydroxide (caustic soda) is a very powerful cleaner cum steriliser. Cleaners used by commercial breweries are based upon sodium hydroxide plus sodium hypochlorite. The detergent supplied to pubs for use in automatic glass washers is usually nothing other than a 3% to 5% solution of caustic soda. Caustic soda in its powder form is pretty nasty corrosive stuff, but if used wisely it can save an awful lot of scrubbing. Stubborn deposits in the bottoms of bottles, or the yeasty ring around the inside of a demijon are typical occasions when I have resorted to using a hot solution of caustic soda. One tablespoon in a gallon of hot water is sufficient for our applications. Caustic soda is most effective when hot, and a fifteen minute soak is sufficient. Items cleaned in caustic soda will need to be very thoroughly rinsed afterwards. Do not use it on aluminium. Read the safety precautions on the side of the container. Take care not to get the solution on your skin or splash it into your eyes.

Chempro SDP

Chempro SDP is a commercial multi purpose cleaning and sterilising agent supplied in powder form. It is inexpensive, very economical to use, and available in all home brew shops. Recommended usage is two teaspoonsful per gallon or per five litres in warm (not boiling) water. Items to be cleaned should be left to soak for about 20 minutes. Chempro SDP releases chlorine, so the cleaned items require thorough rinsing with cold water to remove all traces. Chempro SDP has better rinsing properties than household bleach.

Sodium metabisulphite

Sodium metabisulphite is one of the most useful substances employed in home brewing. Sodium metabisulphite releases sulphur dioxide, which is a good defence against infecting organisms, but not as good as chlorine based sterilisers. However, sodium metabisulphite has various other useful properties; it will kill most of our spoilage organisms to be found in our beer and yet leave our yeast unharmed; it is an anti-oxidant thus, its presence in beer is advantageous. Potassium metabisulphite has similar properties. Sodium metabisulphite has no cleaning power, but, nevertheless, it is successfully used as the sole sterilising aid by many home brewers.

10% solution of sodium met. is more than adequate for general sterilisation duties, that is 50 grams of powder made up to 500ml with water (2 ounces made up to a pint). Keep it in a washing up liquid bottle, or a garden spray bottle. The concentrated spray is useful for the quick sterilisation of certain items, such as hydrometers or thermometers, or for spraying the inside of a fermentation bin prior to use.

Acidified sodium met.
The addition of an acid to a sodium met. solution will increase its effectiveness as a steriliser by forcing it to release more sulphur dioxide. Half a teaspoonful of citric acid added to one litre of 10% solution is a suitable concentration. Acidified sodium met. should be made up prior to use, as it is not very stable, it will not keep for any length of time as a stock solution.

Sterilising brewing equipment

Probably the easiest method of sterilising all of the bits and bobs employed for brewing is to throw them all into a brewing bin along with about 1 litre of sterilising solution. Ensure that all the items are wetted by the solution, then fit the lid to the bin and leave for about 20 minutes for the vapour to do the sterilising. It is important that the **inside** of syphon tubes and taps are sterilised as well as the outsides. If a chlorine based steriliser is used, very thorough rinsing must follow to remove all traces of chlorine, a spray with the stock sodium met. solution after rinsing, followed by a further rinse will help to remove the chlorine. If sodium met. is the sole sterilising agent rinsing is not so important, the items can be simply left to drain.

Cleaning brewing equipment

Cleaning, as opposed to simply sterilising, often requires a bit more work. Items will need to be totally immersed (not simply wetted) in Chempro SDP, a bleach solution, or a caustic soda solution for a period of of about twenty minutes, scrubbed clean, and rinsed. Sodium met. is not a cleaner, and should not be used for such purpose.

The cleaning of really dirty bottles can be aided by using a piece of lamp chain, or a few small stones and swirling this around inside the bottle.

Brewing equipment

14 Recipe Formulation

'This brewing produces 2 barrels and a half from a quarter. Best pale malt and pocket hops are used at the rate of 6lbs to the quarter. Turn on first mash at 180 degrees and second at 190 degrees. Pitch the tun at 60 degrees and cleanse at 80 degrees. Mash successively one hour and three-quarters of an hour, standing one-and-a-half and two hours. Add in the tun 2lbs yeast fore every barrel and coat with salt and flour after first skimming. After second mash, turn on for table beer at 150 degrees.'

A recipe for RINGWOOD ALE, c1800

Before entering deeply into recipe formulation, it would be well to discuss the beers of old. Modern breweries do not produce the range and quality of beers that were available 50 years ago, therefore our examples must come from the beers of old. Home brewing enables us to produce quality ales without the worry of commercial considerations.

The following price list is for Thomas Parsons, Lion Steam Brewery, Princes Risborough, of around 1890. The prices are per barrel (36 Gallons). For those of you too young to remember; 56/— is equivalent to £2.80 in modern money.

TABLE 14.1

		Brl
XXXX	Strong ale	56/—
XXX	Lighter ditto	48/—
XX	Mild ditto	36/—
XK	Dinner ditto	42/—
X	Kitchen ditto	28/—
T	(at Brewery, not finding casks)	10/—
SKB	Highly recommended	40/—
KB	Ditto	36/—
BA	Fine strong bitter	56/—
Stout	Very nutritious	56/—
Porter		36/—

This table shows by example the range of beers supplied by a typical brewery at the turn of this century. Find a brewery today which supplies ten different cask beers, plus a very weak table beer for which one took their own vessel to the brewery to have filled. Better still, find a brewery which will supply T beer at 1.4 pence per gallon!

TYPES OF ENGLISH BEER

Entire

Although being one of the first of the famous beers (1722), the mere mention of 'Entire' or 'Porter' is enough to drive any brewing historian to drink! All of the large London porter breweries kept their methods and recipes a closely guarded secret, and, for this reason, comparatively little is known about its development. I have several contemporary recipes for entire or porter, but they are so wildly different from each other that each can be classed as a completely different drink. The probable reason for this is, that over the one hundred and fifty years or so of porter's popularity, the drink evolved considerably. Furthermore, the cloak of secrecy surrounding this black gold probably forced many brewers to independently develop their own versions.

Porter from the huge London porter breweries was a high quality drink, in fact a blend of three beers of different ages blended at the brewery. Huge aging vats were constructed by these breweries to age several months supply of beer. In 1814 one of these vats, holding three quarters of a million gallons, burst at the Meux brewery in London killing eight people. Liquorpond street, where the Meux brewery once stood, was possibly named after this event.

Smaller breweries, without the resources to build these huge aging vats, cashed in on the porter phenomena by developing their own 'taste-alike' recipes for a drink which they called porter or entire but without the aging and blending process. Furthermore, porter's heyday was during a period when the duty on beer was levied by means of a malt tax. Obviously, there were many attempts to cheapen a beer by using sources of fermentable material which fell outside the scope of the malt tax, or to give the impression of strength and body to a weak beer by the use of herbs and spices. This, I hope, will go some way to explain why the subject of Entire or Porter is so woolly.

Originally, London porter owed its flavour to the use of very highly coloured black malts, with a major portion of the fermentable material being provided by molasses; which probably fell outside the malt tax for a while. Unmalted roast barley, root liquorice, capsicum (chili), and tartaric acid figured strongly in some of the early recipes. In time the proportion of black malt was considerably lowered due to its low fermentable extract and the deficiency was made up by amber malts. Colour was then prepared by boiling molasses until it was dark bitter and thick, and then setting it on fire and burning it for five or six minutes!

In time the standard porter grist became equal parts of brown, amber, and pale malts with a small quantity of black malt and roast barley added.

Mild ale

The term 'mild' refers to a beer that is mildly hopped, not necessarily weak. The origin of mild probably stems from country brewers attempts at producing a beer to match the London brewers entire. However, mild was a quite different drink, but, being cheap, dark, fairly sweet and flavoursome it soon gained fairly wide acceptance and eventually began to challenge the popularity of London brewed entire. In the course of time the London brewers took up brewing mild. Mild, having no aging and blending process, was cheaper and easier to brew than entire and mild gradually replaced entire.

A modern day dark mild would consist perhaps of equal parts amber and pale malts, plus 5% to 10% Torrified barley, about 15% invert sugar, and a small quantity of black malt. A quality of malt called mild ale malt is also available, which could be substituted for the amber and pale.

Stout

Originally, stout was a stronger version of porter if you lived in London, or a stronger version of mild if you lived in the country. In time, when many breweries produced a porter and a Mild, Stout came to mean a stronger version of mild and 'extra stout' a stronger version of entire. London (and Dublin) extra stouts were high quality beers, being blends of three beers of different ages brewed in a similar manner to entire. Guinness still is I believe.

For some reason it became generally accepted that Stout was very nutritious. This dubious knowledge spawned a whole range of so called food stouts: Invalid stout, Milk Stout, Oatmeal Stout, Oyster stout, and various other variations were marketed on their supposed nutritive benefit.

Stock Ale

In days of old when knights were bold and refrigerators weren't invented; it was not possible to brew good quaffing ale during the summer months, due to problems with infection. To alleviate this problem many astute brewers produced a very strong ale of up to O.G. 1.110. This ale was brewed all year round, except in very hot weather, and put into store. Its very high strength and hop content kept it sound. During the summer, stock ale, which had been brewed during the winter and had matured and aged for several months, was blended with (or diluted by) a very weak freshly brewed beer before being sent to the pub as quaffing ale. The keeping properties of the matured stock ale apparently protected the blended beer, and, of course, reduced the maturation time to almost zero. Beers produced in this manner were ready for consumption within a couple of days of blending and could therefore be drunk about three weeks earlier than conventionally brewed beers. This blending technique apparently increased the shelf life of weak beers considerably, and beers produced in this manner were known as 'keeping beers'. Thomas Parsons' price list, printed at the beginning of this chapter, contains three beers with a 'K' in its title; It is probable that these beers were produced by the blending technique, the KB signifying 'Keeping Beer', SKB 'Strong Keeping Beer'. Some breweries name their mild 'AK', (Ale, Keeping?).

Anyway, back to stock ale; stock ale brewed during the summer often appeared on the pub counter during the winter as strong 'old ale', a tradition which some brewers still maintain.

Ales, beers, bitter

In England there seems to be little or no distinction between the terms ale and beer. Traditionally, brewers name their strong quality products ale and their weak inferior products beer! Some people will argue that, originally, beer was a hopped beverage, and ale was unhopped. However, this is almost certainly not true! The Old English word 'Beor', and the Old Norse word 'Bjorr', supposedly the origin of the word 'beer', was around a few thousand years before the world began to throw hops into their beer. So was Pliny The Elder, who first recorded the use of 'Beor' in England, when the Romans first landed in Kent during the first century A.D. The Danish 'Hall Of Odin' supplied Bjorr to the warrior heroes that were invited therein. If you turn to your Chambers Dictionary you will notice that the origin of the word 'barley' is attributed to the Old English 'baerlic'. It does not take much imagination to mutate 'baer' into beer; after all, we are going back a few thousand years! QED. Now you are lumbered with the assumption that any beverage fermented from barley is generically termed baer, beer, bier, or bjoor; the assumption is almost certainly correct.

On the other hand, the word 'ale' is a much later word, possibly derived from 'alt' meaning high. The Germans have their dark alts (ales) brewed in the north using top working yeasts, and their biers, brewed in the south using bottom working yeasts. Thereby lies a clue to the original meaning of 'ale' (high yeast). The Chambers Dictionary's definition of ale is thus:

'Name applied to beers in brewing of which yeast ferments on top of the liquid.'
And of beer:
'An alcoholic beverage made by fermentation, in which the yeast settles to the bottom.'

Forgetting matters of opinion as to the difference between an ale and a beer; it is generally accepted that ales are higher quality than beers, use less adjuncts or sugar, and are usually sweeter.

It is argued that the highest quality ales are made from malt and hops entirely with no other ingredients. This is certainly true. However, the use of adjuncts does widen the scope of experimentation and allow the production of an ale or beer with a distinctive flavour. A modern beer grist would consist mainly of pale malt, about 10% crystal malt, and probably 5% brewers wheat flour. About 15% invert sugar, or brewing syrup added to the copper is typical. Torrified barley is a common adjunct, and wheat malt is popular in the more recent recipes.

Typical gravities and hop rates

Table 14.2 shows typical original gravities, grist to sugar ratios, and hop rates for the more popular beers of about 60 years ago. The original gravities are somewhat higher than is typical today. The hops column has been adjusted to be equivalent to Goldings hops per 25 litre home-brew batch at the gravity specified. WBC is the equivalent Wheeler Bitterness Constant to be discussed later.

TABLE 14.2

	O.G.	sugar	hops*	WBC
Stock ale	1085	15%	262g.	594
Stout	1055	Nil	143g.	501
Bitter	1055	15%	148g.	518
Mild	1050	15%	97g.	370
Porter	1040	Nil	85g.	409
Light ale	1033	25%	66g.	385

* This is an indication of the quantity of Goldings hops required for a 25 litre batch of the same original gravity. Incidently, Shannon's 'Practical Brewing' of 1805 gives the following typical original gravities: Stock ale 1110, Common ale 1080, porter 1080, and Table beer 1050.

Extraction rates

For every kilogramme of grist that we mash, or every kilogramme of sugar that we add to the copper, we would expect a certain amount of fermentable material to be present in our wort to provide strength.

The following table shows typical laboratory extract rates that are obtainable from our brewing materials when mashing. The figures are in brewer's degrees per kilogram litre; This means that, if one kilogram of pale malt is mashed to produce

1 litre of wort, then, from the table, the theoretical maximum original gravity would be 1.297, or 297 degrees. If the same quantity of malt is mashed to produce two litres of wort, the yield would be half of the previous figure, ie, O.G 1.1485, or 148.5 degrees.

It should be borne in mind that these are **laboratory extracts**, and in practice these figures are not achieved during brewing. The results we get are dependant upon our mash efficiency. Most commercial brewers only achieve a mash efficiency of about 85%. In the home brew environment we may achieve about 80% for strong beers rising to about 85% to 90% for weak beers. More about this later.

TABLE 14.3

	Laboratory extract	Diastatic Power
Pale malt	297	High
Mild ale malt	293	High
Amber malt	280	Medium
Crystal malt	268	Zero
Chocolate malt	268	Zero
Black malt	265	Zero
Lager malt	297	High
Roast barley	270	Zero
Wheat flour	304	Zero
Malted wheat	279	Medium
Flaked wheat	279	Zero
Flaked Barley	253	Zero
Torrified barley	253	Zero
Flaked maize	313	Zero

Note: All extracts are given in brewers degrees per kilogram litre.

When formulating a recipe we should assume that we have a mash efficiency of 80%, and a wort loss of about 10%, unless we have more accurate figures taken from practical experience with our equipment. It is far better to have too much wort and throw some away, than have too little, such that our barrel has too much air space. Therefore to end up with a 25 litre batch of beer we will need to brew 27.5 litres, or if our batch length is 23 litres (5 gallons) we will need to begin with 25 litres.

To use the above tables:

$$Lab\ Extract \times quantity \times O.G. = \frac{mash\ efficiency}{Volume\ being\ brewed \times 100}$$

Note: O.G. in brewers degrees, ie 1044 = 44.

Therefore 5 Kg of pale malt at 80% mash efficiency, and a 25 litre final volume (27.5 litres initial), will yield:

$$O.G. = \frac{297 \times 5 \times 80}{27.5 \times 100} = 43.2 \quad (OG = 1043.2)$$

If we brew a beer from 5 Kg of pale malt, we can assume that about 20% residual dextrins will remain in our beer after fermentation, therefore, our final gravity can be calculated as:

$F.G. = 43.2 \times 0.2 = 1008.6$

The quantity of pale malt required to produce a beer of a desired gravity can be found by:

$$Qty \; of \; malt = \frac{O.G. \times Volume \times 100}{Lab \; extract \times Mash \; efficiency}$$

For a 25 litre batch at 1055, this equates to:

$$Qty \; of \; malt = \frac{55 \times 27.5 \times 100}{297 \times 80} = 6.36 \; Kg$$

The following table shows the extract obtained from sugars and syrups which are not mashed, they are added directly to the copper. Mash efficiency does not apply and we get the full extract from these ingredients. Also note that the ingredients marked * are 100% fermentable, leave no residual extract or sweetness in the beer, and make no contribution to final gravity.

TABLE 14.4

	Diastatic Extract	Power
Malt extract	300	Varies, Zero to high
White sugar	*360	Zero
Brown sugar	*330	Zero
Invert sugar	*288	Zero
Glucose	*360	Zero
Corn syrup	300	Zero
Barley syrup	300	Varies

Hop utilisation

It is impossible to give precise figures regarding hop utilisation. Apart from the fact that bitterness and flavour of a beer are subjective assessments, different varieties of hop impart different degrees of bitterness and also different flavours and aromas. Some varieties of hop are twice as bitter as other varieties, and the flavour and aroma of some varieties of hop are attractive whereas with other varieties of hop it is objectionable.

It is usual for a home brewing book to supply a hop utilisation table, but in general they are quite meaningless. Different types of hop will produce quite different results. How bitter should a bitter be? One recent author goes as far as stating that a 1040 bitter **requires** 1lb of hops per barrel. Such statements, without further qualification, are absolute rubbish! For example, Target hops are 2.5 times more bitter than Fuggles, meaning that 60% less Target hops could be

TABLE 14.5

| | Typical hop constituents (%) | | | | |
| | Alpha | Beta | Essential | | |
Hop Type	Acid	Acid	Oils	% Crop	Type
Target					
(seeded)	11.2	5.2	1.36	26.5	C
(seedless)	11.7	— —	1.63	2.4	C
Yeoman	10.6	5.2	1.03	8.4	C
Zenith					
(seeded)	9.0	3.3	1.36	1.44	C
(seedless)	9.5	— —	1.98	0.30	C
Omega	9.7	4.0	1.12	0.15	C
Challenger	7.7	3.9	0.97	14.9	D
Northdown					
(seeded)	8.0	5.2	1.23	12.0	D
(seedless)	10.3	— —	1.96	1.9	D
Northern	7.6	5.0	0.97	1.2	D
Brewer					
Bullion	7.9	5.2	1.18	2.7	D
Golding	5.3	2.5	0.77	11.0	A
Fuggle	4.5	2.5	0.66	10.0	A
W.G.V.	6.3	2.6	0.92	3.3	A
Bramling	6.2	2.5	0.91	1.4	A
Cross					
Progress	6.2	2.5	0.65	1.4	A
Other				1.0	

This table is compiled from information kindly supplied by English Hops Limited.

NOTE: Figures are for seeded varieties unless otherwise stated.

Figures are typical only and vary from harvest to harvest.

C = copper or alpha hops, D = general purpose hops, A = aroma hops used to achieve the same degree of bitterness. Needless to say, the flavour and aroma imparted would also be quite different. Furthermore lbs per barrel are not units with which a typical home brewer is particularly accustomed to working.

The bitterness of a hop is judged by its alpha-acid content. Immediately after hops are harvested, the percentage alpha-acid content of every batch of hops is measured and this information is supplied to the commercial purchaser as the basis on which to determine the quality of the hops, comparative hopping rates, and ultimately the market price of the hops. Obviously if a batch of hops has 20% lower alpha-acid content than the previous batch, the brewer will need to use more hops (25% more) to achieve the same bitterness in his beer and will obviously not be prepared to pay as high a price for them. The other constituents, beta-acids and essential oils, are considered to be present in the same ratios, therefore in this particular case they would also be 20% down on the norm.

The table on page 128 provides typical hop constituents, percentage of total U.K. crop, and the hop classification.

All of these varieties of hop are available to the home brewer via good home brewing suppliers. The table is useful if we wish to experiment by using a different variety of hop than is specified in a particular recipe. It can be seen that Target has a much higher alpha-acid content than does Fuggles, and is therefore much more bitter. Obviously, if we were replacing Fuggles with Target, considerably less Target hops would be employed to achieve the same degree of bitterness. Commercial breweries are able to balance their bitterness in terms of Alpha Acid Units by measurement. This is out of the scope of all but the keenest home brewer.

The optimum bitterness of a home brewed beer is determined primarily by beer type, and secondarily by personal preference. It is obvious that a bitter should be much more bitter than a mild, and an ale should probably be somewhere between the two. However, a strong bitter would need more hops to balance the malty sweetness than a weak bitter, and likewise a strong mild would need more hops than a weak mild.

In order to make the hopping rates of home brewed beers, during experimentation or recipe formulation, a relatively painless process, I have devised a simple empirical formula which is designed to take most of the variables into account. Enter the **W**heeler **B**itterness **C**onstant!

You can calculate the Wheeler Bitterness Constant for your favourite home brewed beer thus:

$$Bitterness\ Constant = \frac{weight\ of\ hops \times alpha\text{-}acid\ percent}{beer\ gravity \times volume\ brewed}$$

Note: Weight of hops in grams
Alpha acid in %

Beer gravity in brewers degrees (ie, 1044 = 44)
Volume brewed in litres

Therefore, if your favourite beer was brewed as a 25 litre batch, had a gravity 1044, and used 120 grams of Golding hops having an alpha-acid content of 5.3%, The Wheeler Bitterness Constant would be:

$$WBC = \frac{120 \times 5.3}{44 \times 25} = 0.578$$

The higher the bitterness constant, the more bitter the beer tastes.

If several different types of hop are being employed in the recipe, the bitterness constant for each type of hop can be calculated individually, and the total bitterness constant can be found by adding the individual bitterness constants together.

If, however, we wished to brew a similar beer, but using a different variety of hop, having an alpha-acid content of only 4%, the new quantity of hops required can be obtained thus:

$$weight\ of\ hops = \frac{WBC \times volume \times gravity}{alpha\text{-}acid\ value}$$

$$Hops\ required = \frac{0.578 \times 25 \times 44}{4} = 159\ grams$$

The same formula can be used if you wished to brew a different volume of beer, or a beer of a different gravity having the same relative hopping rate, by simply changing the volume or gravity figure in the formula to the new value, maintaining the bitterness constant the same.

For those that have not yet found a favourite home brewed beer, table 14.2 provides typical Wheeler Bitterness Constants for the popular types of beer. You will eventually devise your own table of bitterness constants for the various types of beer that you brew.

The method can only be regarded as approximate, because not only does the alpha acid content of hops vary (slightly) from season to season, but also with the age and storage conditions of the hop. Commercial brewers blend hops of different ages in order to try to maintain consistency in their beers.

Practical Example

Now to put what we have learned so far into practice. We will produce 25 litres of a 1045 bitter using a grist of 70% pale malt, 10% crystal malt, 5% wheat flour, plus 15% invert sugar (in the copper). We will assume an 80% mash efficiency and a 10% wort loss. We will use Challenger hops.

As a starting point we calculate the TOTAL grist required in terms of pale malt, because all of the extracts are fairly similar. To compensate for the 10% wort loss we will need to start with 27.5 litres of beer.

$$Qty = \frac{44 \times 27.5 \times 100}{297 \times 80} = 5.09 \text{ Kg}$$

Then as a first stab break the 5.09 kg into the respective ratios, thus:

70% Pale malt   = 5.09 × 0.7 = 3.560 Kg
10% Crystal Malt = 5.09 × 0.1 = 0.509 Kg
 5% Wheat flour = 5.09 × 0.05 = 0.025 kg
15% Invert Sugar = 5.09 × 0.15 = 0.763 Kg

Now we have an approximate grist makeup in the correct ratios, but the snag is that although the extracts from all of the ingredients are fairly similar, the pale malt, wheat flour and crystal malt are placed in the mash tun, and are subject to the mashing efficiency figures and respective wort losses; whereas the invert sugar is not. So now we work backwards, using the extraction rates from the tables, to see how close to O.G. 1045 we really are.

Pale malt: 3.560 ×   297   1057
Crystal malt: 0.509 × 268 136
Wheat flour: 0.025 × 304 8

– – – –

Cereal total   1201

$$Cereal \; extract = \frac{1201 \times 80}{27.5 \times 100} = 34.9 \; brewers \; degrees$$

Now for the invert sugar calculation. Notice that sugar is not affected by our mashing efficiency so the 80/100 comes out of the equation:

$$Invert \; sugar: \frac{0.763 \times 288}{27.5} = 7.8 \; brewers \; degrees$$

From this, our total extract is 42.7 degrees (34.9 + 7.8),which is down upon our requirements. Now:

$$\frac{Target \; Gravity}{Actual \; Gravity} = \frac{45}{42.7} = 1.05$$

If we now go and multiply the quantities of all our ingredients by 1.05 and round up to a convenient figure, our beer will be as near as soddit to specification. In fact such a small adjustment is probably not necessary, bearing in mind that we have made a generous allowance for mash efficiency. However it is better to err on the high side. Having done the adjustment; the contribution from the malt will be 36.7 degrees, and from the sugar 8.3 degrees, giving us our 1045 as specified.

Now for the hops:

We have agreed to use Challenger hops, which, by table 14.5, have an alpha-acid content of 7.7%. Table 14.2 suggests that a WBC of 0.518 is typical for a bitter. Thus, from the formula above:

$$Hops\ required = \frac{0.518 \times 27.5 \times 45}{7.7} = 83\ grams$$

Final gravity can be estimated by multiplying the extract contributed from the malt by between 0.20 and 0.25 thus final gravity will be:

$36.7 \times 0.25 = 9.2$

It is important that the contribution from the sugar is not included in this calculation, because invert sugar is 100% fermentable.

Probable alcohol content can be estimated thus:

$$\frac{O.G - F.G.}{7.4} = \frac{4 - 9.2}{7.4} = 4.8\%\ alcohol$$

15 Malt Extract Beers

Partial mash

It is possible to produce simple beers from malt extract without mashing, a technique known as simple brewing. Simple brewing has the disadvantage that we are limited in the range of ingredients that can be used in our beers. Apart from malt extract, the only ingredients that we are able to use without mashing are crystal malt, black malt and chocolate malt. There are a number of other ingredients which are unavailable to us when we employ the simple brewing method, because these other ingredients need to be mashed in order to extract the fermentable material.

A solution to this problem is to use a technique known as the partial mash. In the partial mash, we still use malt extract as our primary source of fermentable extract, but we invoke a simple mash to extract the fermentable material and flavouring from our adjuncts. The partial mash is easier to perform, and is not as critical as a full mash, it is only necessary to hold our wort at approximately 65°C for a period of fifteen minutes to half an hour.

A source of enzymes is necessary to affect the conversion of our adjuncts, and for this we mash our adjuncts alongside a type of malt extract known as **diastatic malt syrup**. This is malt extract in which the diastatic enzymes have not been destroyed by the manufacturing process. It is important to understand that not all types of malt extract are diastatic. The two best known types of diastatic malt extract are manufactured by EDME, called Edme DMS, and Edme SFX. Contrary to the implication given by the names of the two extracts, SFX has a much higher diastatic power than does DMS, although both are adequate for our purposes. Your home brew supplier will ensure that he provides you with a diastatic extract if you ask him nicely. In general, if it does not say diastatic on the container, then assume that it isn't.

In general, most diastatic malt extracts can be used to convert about 20% of their weight of additional adjuncts. As most adjuncts are used in fairly small proportions, this figure is ample. The starch end point test can be used to ensure that conversion is complete. It is good practice to add half a teaspoonful of calcium sulphate, and half a teaspoonful of magnesium sulphate to the mash, although not always necessary. If your boiler has not got a false perforated bottom, then you will also need a bag to hold the hops, else they will block the tap when you come to run off. Adjuncts can either be added freely to boiler or contained in a bag as you wish, if they are added freely to the boiler, then a strainer will be required when running off.

Partial mash technique

1). Put about 18 litres (4 gallons) of water into the boiler and heat to about 40°C. Stir in the malt extract and other grains, but not sugar or hops. Add one teaspoonful of calcium carbonate and half a teaspoon of magnesium sulphate.

2). **Very slowly** raise the temperature to 65°C and hold there for about 15 minutes. Stir frequently. Monitor carefully and try to maintain 65°C for this 15 minute standing period. Ensure that the temperature does not exceed 70°C. Cold water can be added to lower the temperature in an emergency.

3). When the standing period has elapsed, **slowly** raise the temperature to 75°C, and then to boiling point as fast as you wish.

4). When the wort is boiling add the hops and sugars called for in the recipe. Copper finings can be added at this stage if desired. Boil vigorously for about 45 minutes.

5). Switch off the boiler. Strain off the wort from the hops and other grains into a fermenting bin. Sparge the spent grains and hops with a couple of kettles full of hot water, no more.

6). When cooled to room temperature, adjust to the desired original gravity with cold water and then add the yeast. Maintain fermentation between the limits of 18°C and 22°C

Dropping

After the beer has been fermenting for about two days, the beer should be transferred to a secondary fermentation vessel, and fermentation should be completed in this. Care should be taken to ensure that as much debris as possible is left behind in the original vessel, and to admit the minimum of air into solution during the transfer. The beer is ready for racking when the beer reaches final gravity. The lid can be fitted to the bin for protection when the fermentation velocity abates. Racking and finishing are covered elsewhere in this opus.

Simple recipes (no mashing required)

The following is a collection of simple malt extract recipes using ingredients that do not require mashing, ie the temperature hold at 65°C in the boiler is not required.

Strawlight 25 L.

Malt extract	1600 g	Original gravity	1035
White sugar	1100 g	Final gravity	1005
Golding hops	63 g		

Amberlight 25 L.

Malt extract	1100 g	Original gravity	1034
Crystal Malt	600 g	Final gravity	1004
White sugar	1100 g		
Goldings Hops	60g		

Manchester Mild *A good dry mild* 25 L.

Malt extract	2200 g	Original gravity	1040
Crystal malt	440 g	Final gravity	1007
Black malt	100 g		
Brown sugar	700 g		
Fuggle hops	80 g		

Sweet Geordie Brown *Good strong brown* 25 L.

Malt extract	3200 g	Original gravity	1048
Crystal Malt	250 g	Final gravity	1010
Black malt	100 g		
Brown sugar	500 g		
Northern Brewer hops	80 g		

Brainbetter Bitter *A light thin bitter* 25 L.

Malt extract	1100 g	Original gravity	1034
Crystal malt	550 g	Final gravity	1004
Black malt	30 g		
Goldings hops	80 g		

Barleybyte Bitter *Premium best bitter* 25 L.

Malt extract	3200 g	Original gravity	1044
Crystal malt	250 g	Final gravity	1009
Brown sugar	250 g	Dry hops (Golding)	10 g
Fuggle hops	60 g		
Golding hops	30 g		

Bubblesort Bitter *Premium best bitter* 25 L.

Malt extract	3200 g	Original gravity	1046
Crystal malt	250 g	Final gravity	1009

White sugar	250 g	Dry hops (Goldings)	10 g
Molasses	100 g		
Fuggle hops	60 g		
Golding hops	30 g		

Algorithm Ale *Strong dark ale 25 L.*

Malt extract	4000 g	Original gravity	1052
Crystal malt	450 g	Racking gravity	1010
Black malt	100 g		
Fuggle hops	100 g		

PARTIALLY MASHED BEERS

The following is a selection of recipes for partially mashed beers. Only a few recipes have been given because the partial mash brewer is able to use any of the full mash recipes given in the next chapter by substituting a quantity equal to 80% of diastatic malt extract for the pale malt or mild ale malt given in the recipes.

Farmers Ale *A light bitter 25 L.*

DMS malt extract	1700 g	Original gravity	1038
Flaked barley	230 g	Final gravity	1006
Crystal malt	230 g		
White sugar	900 g		
Golding hops	60 g		

Bitter *A quality bitter 25 L.*

DMS malt extract	2500 g	Original gravity	1040
Crystal malt	200 g	Racking gravity	1008
Malted wheat	60 g		
Flaked barley	250 g		
White sugar	350 g		
Golding hops	85 g		

Best Bitter *A quality bitter 25 L.*

DMS malt extract	2800 g	Original gravity	1045
Crystal malt	200 g	Racking gravity	1009
Flaked maize	400 g		
White sugar	350 g		
Fuggle hops	60 g		
Golding hops	60 g		

Celebration ale *Strong old ale 25 L.*

DMS malt extract	3200 g	**Original gravity**	1055
Crystal malt	350 g	**Final gravity**	1012
Flaked maize	350 g		
Roast barley	120 g		
Black malt	120 g		
Demorara sugar	450 g		
Challenger hops	60 g		
Fuggle hops	60 g		

Genius substitute *Irish stout 25 L.*

DMS malt extract	3200 g	**Original gravity**	1045
Flaked barley	250 g	**Racking gravity**	1010
Roast barley	400 g		
Challenger hops	30 g		
Northdown hops	90 g		

Pitching the yeast

16 Making mashed beers

Preliminary work

A few days before you plan to brew your main batch of beer; make up a yeast starter and perform your normal water treatment for the type of beer being brewed. Aerate the treated water and store it in a five gallon barrel until you are ready to use it.

Mash liquor

Put 25 litres of treated water into the brewing boiler and heat it to about 4°C above strike heat (about 77°C). When the liquor is up to temperature run about 15 litres into the mash tun. Put the lid on the mash tun and wait a few minutes for the temperature to stabilise. After a few minutes have elapsed check that the temperature of the mash liquor is at strike heat (about 72°C). Adjust the temperature if necessary by adding boiling or cold water.

The mash

When you have assured yourself that the temperature of the mash liquor is at strike heat, carefully add the grist and stir it into the liquor taking care to ensure that there are no dry pockets. Stir until you are perfectly sure that there are no dry pockets remaining, else an inefficient mash will result. Then measure the temperature of the mash to ensure that it is at initial heat (approx 66°C). If the mash is not at the proper temperature, quickly adjust it to its correct temperature by adding boiling or cold water and stirring it well into the mash. Fit the lid, and cover it with some insulation. Leave it to stand for about one and a half hours or an appropriate mashing period. Monitor the temperature of the mash periodically, if the temperature falls by more than about 3 or 4°C, correct it by adding boiling water and stirring it well in. This should not be necessary if the mash tun is properly insulated.

While the mash is in progress, ensure that there is sufficient water in the boiler for sparging, and set the thermostat on the boiler to maintain the sparge liquor at a temperature of 77°C to 80°C

Running-off

After the mash has stood for the desired length of time, usually about one and a half hours, carefully open the tap on the mash tun and allow the sweet wort to **slowly** run into a collection vessel, taking care to ensure that the flow is not so fast that the goods in the tun bed down and block. The flow should be very low indeed. The grain should act as a filter bed. The first runnings of the sweet wort will be turbid, and these should be carefully returned to the mash tun until the sweet wort runs bright.

If you have two boilers; one can be used as the collection vessel, while the other heats the sparge liquor. It is desirable that the wort is not allowed to cool between collection and boiling, therefore the thermostat on the collection boiler should be set to about 77°C while collection is in progress. If you only have one boiler, as do most people, then collect in your fermentation vessel and transfer to the boiler as soon as sparging is completed.

Sparging

When the mash tun has been run-off sparging must begin. Which ever sparging method you use, the grains should be rinsed with hot liquor maintained at a temperature of approximately 77°C. The sparge should be a light spray, care should be taken to ensure that the mash bed does not crack. Again this should be performed **Slowly** and **Carefully!**

Monitor the gravity of the spargings and stop sparging when this falls to below about 1005. A common sparging technique does not drain the mash bed completely, but supplies sufficient sparge liquor to keep the mash bed floating. This technique is probably better if a set mash is likely, but it does run the risk of supplying too much matter in suspension to the subsequent processes.

The boil

Once all of the wort has been collected, the copper should be set to full power, and the boil begun. As soon as the wort comes to the boil, any sugars that are used in the recipe are slowly added to the copper, and the first batch of hops are added. A good vigorous boil for a period of about one and a half, to two hours, is required.

About fifteen minutes before the end of the boiling period, the second batch of hops and the Irish moss (if used) is added. When the wort has been boiled for the desired length of time the boiler is switched off and a period is allowed for the trub and hop debris to settle. The wort can then be run into a bin, taking care to ensure that that as much debris as possible is left behind in the copper, filtered by the bed of hops, (if you have a perforated false bottom fitted). A light sparging of the hops will ensure that maximum extract is achieved, but sparging should be very light.

Wort cooling

The wort should be cooled as rapidly as possible by plunging the bin into a sink or bath full of cold water, or by means of cooling apparatus. When the wort has cooled sufficiently, and any further precipitation of trub has settled out, the wort can then be carefully transferred, by means of the tap or a syphon tube, into the fermentation vessel, leaving the trub behind. Alternatively the trub can be filtered out after cooling by means of a piece of muslin or straining bag material placed inside a colander or a winemakers filter funnel and carefully running the wort through it.

Fermentation

Cold water is added to the fermentation vessel to bring the wort to the desired original gravity. When the temperature is between the limits of 18°C to 22°C, the contents of the yeast starter bottle is added and fermentation will begin.

Dropping

After the beer has been fermenting for about two days the beer should be transferred to a secondary fermentation vessel and fermentation completed in this. Care should be taken to ensure that as much debris as possible is left behind in the original vessel, and to admit the minimum of air into solution during the transfer. The lid and an airlock can be fitted to the bin for protection when the fermentation velocity abates. Racking and finishing are covered in previous chapters.

Recipes

I have deliberately kept these recipes free from extraneous clutter, and have omitted details of such things as mash times, mash temperatures, mash pH, and 101 other things; all of which are a matter of individual style. In general, if you strike at 72°C, mash for one and a half hours at 65°C, using 2 to 3 litres of liquor per kilogram of malt, sparge at 77°C to 80°C, and boil for two hours; you will get good results. I will leave you to experiment using different parameters.

The quantities of ingredients listed below are deliberately generous. Many modern home brewing vessels are designed for 25 litres rather than the old 5 gallons (22.5 litres). It is assumed that a 10% wort loss will occur during fermentatiom, yeast skimming, racking, etc. Therefore we will need to make 27.5 litres of beer to end up with a final volume of 25 litres. If your barrel is 5 gallons

(22.5 litres), then the starting volume will be 25 litres, and the ingredients could be reduced by 10% for the same strength beer. Furthermore I have assumed that 80% mashing efficiency will be achieved, which is quite low, but this does make allowance for the possibility of slack malt being used. In practice, with freshly milled malt, you may find that your mashing efficiency well exceeds this figure, and the ingredients can be reduced accordingly.

The best beer in the world 25 L.

Pale malt *Goldings*	5800 g	Original gravity	1055
Copper hops	135 g	Final gravity	1014
Nothing Else!			

Mash Tun Mild 25 L.

Mild ale malt	3500 g	Copper hops *Fuggles*	50 g
Chocolate malt	50 g	Late hops *Fuggles*	10 g
Wheat flour	200 g	Dry hops	None
Invert sugar	700 g	Original Gravity	1040
Final Gravity	1008		

Wheeler's Stout 25 L.

Mild ale malt	4500 g	Copper hops *Fuggles*	80 g
Black malt	50 g	Late hops *Fuggles*	20 g
Roast barley	50 g	Dry hops	None
Wheat flour	200 g	Original gravity	1048
Torrified Barley	250 g	Final gravity	1010
Dark brown sugar	500 g		

Pennine Bitter 25 L.

Pale malt	3000 g	Copper hops *Northdown*	50 g
Crystal malt	200 g	Late hops *Northdown*	12 g
Malted wheat	150 g	Dry hops	None
Invert Sugar	650 g	Original gravity	1035
Irish moss	1 teasp	Final gravity	1007

Black Country Bitter 25 L.

Pale malt	3250 g	Copper hops *North'n brwr*	60 g
Crystal malt	160 g	Late hops *Fuggles*	15 g
Wheat flour	330 g	Dry hops	None
White sugar	425 g	Original gravity	1039
Irish moss	1 teasp	Final gravity	1008

Caroline *Caroline's favourite* 25 L.

Pale malt	3500 g	**Copper hops** *Goldings*	110 g
Crystal malt	350 g	**Late hops**	None
Flaked maize	500 g	**Dry hops**	None
Invert sugar	400 g	**Original gravity**	1041
Irish moss	1 teasp	**Final gravity**	1009

Burton Bitter 25 L.

Pale malt	4000 g	**Copper hops** *Target*	40 g
Crystal malt	400 g	**Late hops** *Goldings*	40 g
Invert sugar	600 g	**Dry hops** *Goldings*	10 g
Irish moss	1 teasp	**Original gravity**	1045
Final Gravity	1010		

XXL S.P.A. 25 L.

Pale malt	4500 g	**Copper hops** *Challenger*	60 g
Crystal malt	250 g	**Late hops** *Goldings*	60 g
Flaked barley	450 g	**Dry hops** *Goldings*	15 g
Brown Sugar	600 g	**Original gravity**	1050
Irish moss	1 teasp	**Final gravity**	1011

Saunderton Stout 25 L.

Amber malt	4000 g	**Copper hops** *Challenger*	70 g
Black malt	100 g	**Original gravity**	1038
Chocolate malt	200 g	**Final gravity**	1009

Wheelers Entire 25 L.

Pale malt	2500 g	**Copper hops** *Goldings*	150 g
Amber malt	2500 g	**Original gravity**	1065
Chocolate malt	2500 g	**Final gravity**	1016
Black malt	400 g		

Genius Irish stout 25 L.

Pale malt	4000 g	**Copper hops** *Northdown*	90 g
Black malt	200 g	**plus** *Challenger*	30 g
Roast barley	500 g	**Original gravity**	1044
Flaked barley	500 g	**Final gravity**	1011

Old Grumpy 25 L.

Pale malt	6000 g	**Copper hops** *Goldings*	160 g
Crystal malt	500 g	**Original gravity**	1072
Chocolate malt	300 g	**Final gravity**	1015
Black malt	300 g		
Brown sugar	1000 g		

Old Dorchester ale 25 L.

Amber malt	4600 g	**Copper hops** *Goldings*	100 g
Chocolate malt	2300 g	**Original gravity**	1055
Final gravity	1013		

An 1800 recipe for 'A good Porter' 25 L.

Mild ale malt	4700 g
Black malt	200 g
Crude black strap *Molasses*	130 g
Sliced liquorice root	110 g
Spanish liquorice	57 g
Tartaric acid	1 heaped teaspoonful
Capsicum	1 small level teaspoonful
Common salt	1 teaspoonful
hops *Goldings*	100 g
Original gravity	1043
Final gravity	1010

The tartaric acid is added to the mash along with the mild ale malt and black malt. All of the other ingredients are added to the copper. Both forms of liquorice and the black strap can be obtained from any good health food shop. Cayenne pepper, and Chili pepper (not chili powder) are types of capsicum.

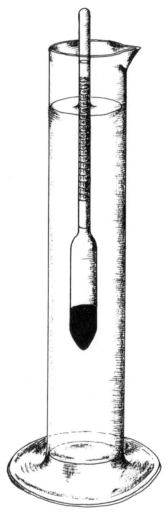

The hydrometer

17 Lager

The word 'lager' is German for store-house; a lager beer is a stored beer and that is all! It matters not whether the beer is pale or dark, fermented by a top working yeast or bottom worker, whether it is infusion mashed or decoction mashed, or whether you drive an XR3i or ride a push bike. The lagering of beer began in Germany for the very same reason that old ales and stock ales were produced in England, specifically; that it was not possible to brew during the summer months, therefore one brewed the summer's supply of beer during the winter and **stored, stocked or lagered** it until the summer. Southern Germany with its higher temperatures and shorter brewing season than England had particular problems and resorted to lagering their beer in deep mountain caves, which maintained very low temperatures.

It is often said that continental lager is traditionally fermented with a strain of bottom working yeast known as *Saccharomyces Carlbergenis*. This is not strictly true. The Bavarians brew with both top working and bottom working yeasts. It is true to say that secondary fermentation is always performed by means of *Saccharomyces Carlbergenis* because it can cope better with the low lagering temperatures than can a top worker. There now seems to be some professional doubt as to whether *Saccharomyces Carlsbergenis* actually exists as an independent strain, it is now thought that it is, in fact, a strain of *Saccharomyces cerivisiae* that has adapted to bottom working through centuries of being expected to work at low temperatures and has been renamed *Saccharomyces Uvarum*.

If a bottom worker is being employed for primary fermentation, fermentation temperature is usually much lower than for ale production and is not usually allowed to rise above about 12°C. Commercially, the fermentation of lager is begun at about 7°C, and the temperature is allowed to gradually rise, reaching about 12°C halfway through fermentation. The fermentation is then cooled, the temperature being lowered to about 7°C by the end of the fermentation period.

The beer is then transfered to an enclosed conditioning tank where the beer is encouraged to go through a secondary fermentation, either using the natural fermentable material and yeast remaining in the beer, or by the addition of a Krausen wort, an actively fermenting wort containing a bottom yeast. At first the carbon dioxide produced by the secondary fermentation is allowed to escape, which purges the unwanted volatiles out of the beer; after which the tank is sealed and the beer becomes carbonated.

Next is the lagering stage. After sufficient time has elapsed for the beer to become carbonated; the temperature of the beer is lowered to around 4°C, and held in this state for about two weeks. This causes much haze forming material, yeast, and protein to sediment out.

The final stage is to lower the temperature to about 0°C to force a chill haze, and then to pump the beer through filters to filter out the haze forming proteins and yeast, before barrelling or bottling.

There are many variations of the techniques employed in the production of lager. Some breweries utilise a diacetyl rest period for a few days at 18°C which reduces the lagering time. Others only lager for a period of 3 or 4 days at 4°C to 7°C. Some don't lager at all. In fact, with modern highly modified malts, I doubt if the lagering process performs any useful function apart from maturation. Traditionally, the Bavarians would lager for about six months.

Lager malt and hops

It is fitting that we clear up a few misconceptions regarding lager malt and the decoction mash. Originally continental malt was less well modified than English malt, and the decoction mash process was developed by the Germans in the late 19th century to overcome clarity problems associated with poorly modified, high nitrogen malts. At the time the Germans probably did not realise that the quality of their barley and their malting technique was the problem. The low temperature protein rest period of the decoction mash or the temperature programmed mash merely completes the malting process. In modern times the Germans have learned from English barley growing and malting experience enabling them to produce well modified, controlled nitrogen level malts, which, ironically, technically made the German decoction mash system redundant. In fact as I write, the larger German breweries are considering adopting the more energy efficient infusion mash process. Remember that the decoction mash was developed in the late 19th century – centuries after lagering began to be practised.

Barley produced in some other countries such as America and Australia, due to the strains of barley employed and the climatic conditions encountered, is high in nitrogen and therefore high in enzymes. It is usual for breweries in these countries to add high levels of unmalted grains such as rice and maize grits to their grist to act as nitrogen dilutents, the enzyme 'proteinase' contained in the malt breaking down undesirable proteins contained in the grits. For these breweries a decoction type of mash system is essential.

The so called 'lager malt' available to home brewers in this country will almost certainly be fully modified making it unnecessary to use the decoction mash or the temperature programmed mash unless high levels of unmalted grains are used in the grist makeup. It is not even necessary to use lager malt, it is in fact preferable to use pale malt if the infusion mash is being employed. In theory lager malt should be richer in enzymes than pale malt, particularly proteinase, due to the lower kilning temperatures involved. It would only be appropriate to use lager malt if a high proportion of unmalted grains were employed in the grist makeup, along with the decoction mash.

Most varieties of English hop are perfectlty suited to the production of lager. This is not surprising when one learns that many so called 'continental hops' are derived from English varieties. This is further illustrated by the fact that nearly 40% of total world hop production is given to varieties of hop developed and bred in England. Hops are difficult to grow and are subject to frequent crop failures. Indeed, a world wide hop market has developed to share the world's hop resources. This means, in a commercial beer at least, that one can not guarantee where the hops were grown, it could change from year to year depending upon which country had the best harvest.

Among the English varieties of hop that have a sufficiently delicate aroma for lager production are: Challenger, Fuggles, Golding, Northdown, Yeoman, and Zenith. It is often said that hops employed for lager production must be seedless varieties. However, this is merely a matter of tradition. It makes no real difference whether seeded or seedless hops are employed.

This book is published by CAMRA, modern lager and CAMRA are not good friends. Most modern lagers are chilled, filtered, and artificially carbonated. In general, it matters not where they are brewed, German, Belgian, or Austrian lager is no better than English brewed lager. However, a few small Bavarian breweries practice traditional methods.

There is no reason why good lager can not be produced using conventional English ale brewing techniques as described in the previous chapter. Brew using light coloured ingredients, preferably malt only, and a low hop rate. Brew using the infusion mash, and top ferment. Before lagering Krausen with an active wort containing a lager yeast, and lager at 4°C for several months!

It may come as a surprise to you to learn that one of Britain's most popular commercial lagers is brewed using pale malt, English hops, and the infusion mash system – albeit filtered and fizzed.

18 Other brewing techniques

'The drink which has come to supply the place of beer has, in general been tea. It is notorious that tea has no useful strength in it, that it contains nothing nutritious, that it besides being good for nothing, has badness in it, because it is well known to produce want of sleep in many cases, and in all cases to shake and weaken the nerves'
(from COTTAGE ECONOMY, William Cobbett.)

Introduction to this chapter.

This chapter outlines various special brewing techniques that are available to the commercial brewer. The majority of these techniques require the addition of commercially manufactured brewing enzymes most of which are currently unavailable to the amateur brewer. It is not suggested that all of these techniques are suitable for the amateur, although they can form the basis of experiment for the inquisitive or experimental mind. What follows is merely included to satisfy one's thirst for information, and to indicate possible future trends in home brewing.

Brewing enzymes

There are a number of commercially manufactured enzymes available to the commercial brewer. They are not currently available to the amateur brewer, mainly because we can brew perfectly good beer without them, and because amateur demand and usage would not be sufficient to make the packaging and distribution of them commercially viable. However, it is quite likely that some enterprising home-brew supplier may package some of the more useful enzymes in the near future, particularly those associated with haze prevention and lite beers.

If you are now throwing up your hands in horror at the thought of 'chemical brewing', please bear in mind that it is not quite what it seems. All of these enzymes are derived from quite natural substances, usually bacteria or fungus, remember that yeast is a fungus. I can see nothing wrong with using enzymes during beer production if it results in an improvement in quality or the development of a different type of drink. Most of these enzymes would normally be present in the wort of a conventional beer, either contributed by the barley or secreted by the yeast or a friendly bacteria. The alternative to using industrial enzymes is to culture the donor bacteria or fungus in the wort, a method that is practised in some countries. Very often enzymes are only added to supplement a deficiency in the natural enzymes.

Winemakers have a bewildering array of enzymes available to them. It would be impossible for amateur winemakers to make some of the popular country wines without them. Commercial winemakers are permitted to add a terrific range of additives to their wine. If certain foreign winemakers were forced to print the ingredients of their wine on the side of the bottle it would read like a chemist's shop price list! Fortunately, commercial brewers have no such freedom, they are heavily restricted as to what they can put into their beer. However, a number of industrial enzymes are permitted, and here they are:

Bacterial alpha-amylase

Bacterial alpha-amylase is produced by the deep fermentation of various strains of the bacterium *Bacillus Subtilis* or *bacillus licheniformis*. Its action and behaviour is very similar to the eqivalent enzyme contained in malted barley and can be used as a direct replacement for it. Needless to say, alpha-amylase is supplied by the malted barley and under normal circumstances additions of industrially produced enzyme are unnecessary. Bacterial alpha-amylase has limited application brewing and is mainly used if poor quality barley is obtained, in high adjunct brewing where the malt has insufficient of the natural enzyme to degrade all of the starch, or if an accident has occoured in the brewhouse which has destroyed the natural enzyme. Bacterial alpha-amylase is normally added to the mash tun.

Fungal alpha-amylase

Fungal alpha-amylase is produced by fermentation by the fungus *Apergillus Orzae*. Although this enzyme is similar to, and is classified as an alpha-amylase, it is quite different from both cereal and bacterial alpha-amylase inasmuch as it will attack *some* of the dextrins, converting them to maltose, thus increasing the fermentability of the wort. This makes the enzyme particularly useful in the production of beers where a higher than normal attenuation is desired. Wort attenuations in excess of 80% can be achieved by the use of Fungal alpha-amylase, compared to attenuations of between 65% and 75% for conventionally brewed beers. Fungal alpha-amylase is often added to the mash tun, but due to its low temperature tolerance the temperature programmed mash is preferable. It is typical to hold the mash at a temperature of between 50°C and 70°C for as long as possible before continuing with the normal mash cycle. The boiling stage destroys the enzyme. Commercial breweries are able to add Fungal alpha-amylase to the fermenter, where it can be employed to reduce the possibility of a starch haze if an accident has occurred during mashing, or to improve a slow fermentation. The enzyme is then destroyed by flash pasteurisation. As home brewers we should be wary of adding certain enzymes after the boiling stage of beer production because we have no method of removing them from the beer afterwards. This has the result that the action of the enzyme may continue in the bottle or barrel which may be detrimental to the finished beer.

Cereal Beta-amylase

Commercially produced beta-amylase is extracted from raw barley making it no different from the beta-amylase usually supplied by the malt (or raw barley) used in normal grist makeup. Obviously the application of commercially produced beta-amylase is limited to high adjunct brewing whereby there is insufficient beta-amylase present in the grist to effect efficient conversion of all of the starch into maltose. under these conditions Beta-amylase is added to the mash tun to supplement the natural enzyme.

Fungal amyloglucosidase

This tongue-twisting mouthful is commercially produced by the culture of the equally large mouthful *Aspergillus niger var. awamori*. Amyloglucosidase has the ability to convert the residual dextrins in the wort into glucose, making it useful in the production of low carbohydrate beers, the production of which is outlined later in this chapter. In the production of low carbohydrate beers the enzyme is added to the fermenter towards the end of primary fermentation after the majority of the natural maltose has been fermented. For home brewers, the use of fungal amyloglucosidase in the fermenter would be difficult to control. We have no method of stopping the enzyme activity when the desired point has been reached, and the enzyme would be carried across to the bottles or barrels where its activity would continue. This may be of no consequence on a low carbohydrate very dry beer where there would be little substrate for the enzyme to work on, but on intermediate types this will produce a beer with too high a level of residual sweetness, or too high a level of yeast activity.

An application of fungal amyloglucosidase which is open to amateur use, is that of priming sugar replacement. In this application very low concentrations of the enzyme are added to finished conventionally brewed beers, the gradual and sustained release of glucose will provide continued condition or an increase of sweetness with age depending upon the quantity of yeast present and the amount of enzyme added.

Fungal Beta glucanase

Beta-glucanase has the ability to breakdown troublesome beta-glucan gums which although present in all worts, are particularly troublesome in worts produced from a grist containing a high proportion of unmalted cereals. Beta-glucans increase wort viscosity which can cause problems with mash tun run-off and can cause a beta-glucan haze. Beta-glucanase is in fact present in malted barley, but cereal beta-glucanase is rapidly destroyed at normal infusion mash temperatures; although some activity is retained during the protein rest period of the decoction or temperature programmed mash. Fungal beta-glucanase is much more temperature stable than cereal, or bacterial derived examples and can be safely employed in the conventional infusion mash.

Protease
Protease is usually extracted from the papain tree and is used as a protein haze preventative for finished beer. Similar products simply called papain have been used by home winemakers for a great many years. However, it is not necessary for winemaker's papain to be particularly well refined. It usually contains a number of water soluble vegatable waxes. Although winemaker's papain will act as a protein or chill haze preventative if used in beer, it will often have the side effect of causing poor head retention. A side effect that is an advantage to winemakers who would not normally expect to find a head on their wine. Brewer's protease is therefore much more highly refined than the winemaker's product.

Bacterial Neutral Proteinase
Bacterial neutral proteinase is manufactured by the fermentation of *bacillus subtilis*, and breaks down undesirable haze forming proteins into soluble peptides and amino acids. Cereal proteinase is contained in brewing malt; lager malt in particular, where the lower kilning temperatures preserve a higher proteinase activity. However, in high adjunct, or raw barley brewing, where there could be a high level of undesirable protein coupled with a deficiency in proteinase, it may be necessary to add proteinase in the form of an industrial enzyme to ensure complete conversion. Normally, proteinase is quickly destroyed at normal mashing temperatures. It is therefore usual to employ a mashing system that features a low temperature protein rest period at a temperature of between about 50°C to 55°C for a period of about one hour. There are, however, temperature stabilised forms of proteinase available, which will work satisfactorily at infusion mash temperatures.

Pullulanase
Pullulanase is a synergistic enzyme, which does nothing on its own, but will increase the effect of other enzymes, amyloglucosidase and beta amylase in particular.

Compound enzymes

There are a number of mixed enzyme systems available to the commercial brewer. These are combinations of enzymes mentioned above, ready blended in the correct proportions necessary to provide optimum performance in specific tasks. **Alphalase**™ is a blend of Alpha-amylase, proteinase, and beta-glucanase, blended in the proper proportions for optimum performance in raw barley brewing. **Amylozyme**™ is a blend of beta-amylase and pullulanase, and is used for high wort attenuation, or low carbohydrate beers. **Panazyme**™ is a blend of various forms of proteinase, blended for maximum effectiveness in breaking down undesirable proteins during the mash.

Alphalase, Amylozyme, and Panazyme are trade names of A.B.M. Brewing and food group limited.

Raw barley brewing

Brewing with very high proportions of raw barley in the grist is an attractive proposition for commercial brewers. Significant gains in economy can be achieved by simply bypassing the maltsters. The use of up to 15% unmalted barley in grist makeup has been practised since the war, but if raw barley is used at levels above about 15% of the total grist, problems soon begin to show themselves. Starch and glucan hazes begin to be formed yeast performance deteriorates due to low levels of assimilable nitrogen, and mash tun run-off is impaired due to too a high proportion of beta-glucan gums being present. Modern science has overcome these problems. By the means of adding industrial enzymes to the mash and by using the decoction mash it is now possible to brew with up to 80% raw barley in the grist. Three enzymes are typically added to the mash: **Bacterial neutral proteinase**; which brings about protein degradation, **Bacterial alpha-amylase**; which breaks down the starch, and **Beta-glucanase**; which breaks down the beta-glucan gums. These three enzymes are available to the commercial brewer ready blended as a compound. A fourth important enzyme **Beta-amylase** is normally supplied in sufficient quantities by the raw barley.

The barley needs to be specially milled such that the husk remains intact to provide a free draining mash bed, yet the endosperm must be adequately crushed to ensure the proper extract is achieved.

It is essential that the mash features a protein rest period. Therefore a decoction or temperature programmed mash is employed. Typically the enzymes are added to the mash at low temperature and the mash is initially held at 55°C for up to two hours for proteolysis to occur. The temperature is then raised to between 63°C and 65°C and held for one and a half hours for saccharification. Finally the temperature is slowly raised (1°C per minute) to 80°C for beta-glucan gum degradation. The rest of process is identical to conventional brewing.

High adjunct brewing

The same rules, mashing techniques, and enzymes as used in raw barley brewing are required for high adjunct brewing. However, the lower level of barley employed could result in a deficiency of the important enzyme **Beta-amylase**. It is conventional in high adjunct brewing to add to the mash, in addition to the three enzymes mentioned above, beta-amylase.

Lite beers

A type of drink that has emerged in recent years is a low carbohydrate type of beer known as 'lite'. In ordinary beers 25% to 30% of the total sugars remain after fermentation in the form of residual dextrins. Technically, a lite beer is one where a substantial proportion of the residual dextrins are also fermented out to yield alcohol. The subject of low carbohydrate beers warrants a detailed discussion, because, if the amateur is able to brew low carbohydrate beers, it may open home brewing to people who suffer from diabetic problems.

The typical composition of a conventionally mashed beer wort would be 65% fermentable sugars, 25% non fermentable sugars, and 10% other bits and pieces. After fermentation the wort would exhibit 65% attenuation. There are various ways of increasing the fermentability of the wort, that is fermenting out some (or most) of the residual dextrins.

A). Extended mash times at low mash temperatures will provide an attenuation of about 70%, with about 18% residual dextrins remaining after fermentation.

B). Cane sugar is 100% fermentable. Therefore, increasing the ratio of cane sugar to malt in the recipe will reduce the residual dextrins at the expense of flavour and quality.

C). Adding Fungal alpha-amylase to the mash tun will increase fermentability to about 80%

D). Adding Fungal alpha-amylase and pullanase to the mash tun, and decoction mashing with a temperature hold in the region of 55°C to 60°C (optimum 58°C) for as long as possible before continuing with the normal mash cycle, will increase fermentability to about 85%

E). Adding amyloglucosidase to the fermenter will increase fermentability to 85% to 90%

Of the five options listed above, option **E** is not suitable for home brewing because we have no way of destroying the enzyme after its action has proceeded far enough. The remaining methods are quite suitable for amateur use providing one is able to obtain the necessary enzymes. A combination of **A**, **B**, and **D** would be the best technique. Malt extract brewers could achieve similar results by adding the enzymes to the malt extract and mashing the extract using partial mash techniques.

Low calorie beers

A low calorie beer is defined as a beer that contains less than two thirds of the calories that one would normally expect to find in a beer of the type. A low carbohydrate beer is not a low calorie beer, because low carbohydrate beers convert the residual sugars to alcohol, which contains nearly as many calories as the original sugar. A low calorie beer must therefore be low in carbohydrate *and* low in alcohol. Low calorie beers are usually produced by brewing to a low original gravity all malt wort, using the low carbohydrate techniques described above. Often the final beer is diluted to reduce the calories to the desired level. Recipe balance is difficult, and the resultant beers do not flavour match an equivalent ordinary beer. Low calorie techniques should not find application in home brewing. They really are a bit of a 'con' in many respects. A low calorie beer is still high in calories, producing a full flavoured low calorie beer is impossible.

Low alcohol beers

Alcohol free beers are usually produced by brewing a conventional beer and then removing the alcohol by means of adsorbants, or distillation. Obviously these techniques are unavailable to the amateur. Low alcohol beers can be produced by making a low original gravity beer of low fermentability, ie, exactly the opposite to low carbohydrate beers. A low fermentability beer would be produced from an all malt wort, with low original gravity, mashed at high temperatures.

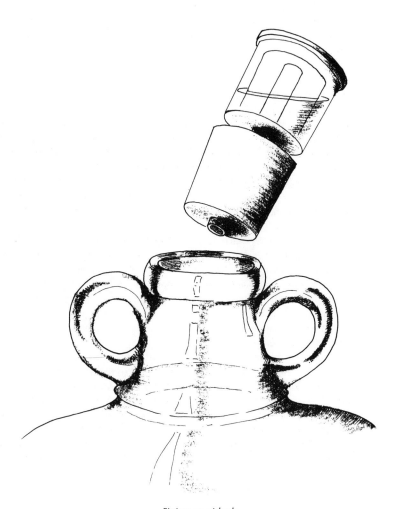

Fitting an airlock

19 Problems

Most people will experience a few problems in their early days of brewing, but most of these can be put down to bad technique. Fortunately, problems with home brewed beer are fairly rare, once one has gained a bit of experience by brewing a few batches. Nevertheless, very occasionally, even experienced brewers will encounter a problem which is difficult to explain.

Poor extraction

I define poor extraction as being a condition where, after mashing and sparging and making up the volume with cold liquor, either the original gravity of the wort, or the final volume is much lower than expected. Poor extraction during the mashing stage of beer production can be caused by a number of problems. The most likely cause is poor quality malt, or slack malt. Ready cracked malt which has been stored in unfavourable conditions can absorb atmospheric moisture and go slack. The other likely problem is incorrect maintenance of mash temperature. If the mash temperature is too low, then an inefficient mash may result, however, this is unlikely to be too much of a problem if the temperature of the mash is returned to its proper value as soon as the error is detected. If the temperature of the mash is allowed to rise too high, then the important enzymes may be destroyed and a poor extraction is sure to result. The pH of the mash could be incorrect, but it would have to be a very long way out to cause poor extraction, and this is unlikely. A further likely cause is inefficient sparging of the grains after the mash. If all other conditions seem okay, then a different sparging method may cure the problem.

Lack of proper yeast head

A common problem is that the yeast does not exhibit the proper top working characteristics associated with a top fermented beer. This could be caused by using an incorrect strain of yeast or too low fermentation temperature. It may be due to poor initial yeast growth caused by too low a level of disolved oxygen in the wort during the early stages of fermentation. A lack of assimilable nitrogen due to poor wort composition is another possibility.

Try raising temperature, aerating the wort, or adding a yeast food. If the problem persists, change your yeast strain.

Slow or poor fermentation

There are a number of reasons for poor fermentation, the problem is identifying the cause. Many of the problems associated with poor fermentation are yeast related, some of these problems covered in the chapter on yeast. Try; rousing the yeast, raising the temperature of the fermentation, adding a yeast food, and as a very last resort – aerating the wort. If the problem persists, change your yeast strain for future brews.

Flat beer

Flat beer is a fault whereby the beer lacks natural condition and sparkle, due to there being insufficient CO_2 in solution. This is caused by either allowing fermentation to proceed too far, to final gravity, if priming is not employed; or insufficient priming sugar if priming is employed. Another probable cause is that the barrel or bottles are not properly sealed, allowing the condition gas to escape. For barrelled beer; try re-priming the beer and allowing a few days for secondary conditioning to take place. Any grease or traces of washing up liquid will cause problems. Recipe formulation can also have a bearing upon the problem.

Gushing

This is exactly the opposite to the condition above, it is a condition where the beer errupts into a mass of foam when dispensed. This is most likely to be caused by bottling or barrelling at too high a specific gravity, or adding too much priming sugar. Remember that beer can be bottled, without adding priming sugars, when the specific gravity is two or three points above final gravity. Alternatively, we can allow fermentation to proceed to final gravity and add priming sugar to generate the secondary condition. Half a teaspoon of sugar per pint, is more than enough. Recipes using high proportions of unmalted grain can also cause gushing.

Poor head retention

Poor head retention is a different condition to flat beer. A beer can have lots of condition and sparkle, but the head will collapse almost immediately. Poor head retention can be caused by allowing greasy or oily substances, detergents or washing-up liquid to come into contact with your beer, glasses, or brewing utensils. If you use washing up liquid or detergents to clean your brewing equipment, the equipment must be very thoroughly rinsed afterwards to remove all traces. Poor head retention can also be caused by the recipe employed. Various consituents in the beer are responsible for the head retention. Beta-glucans, hop resins, and melanoidins aid head retention, whereas hop essential oils and lipids have the opposite effect. Beer viscosity is obviously important. Some types of beer, particularly weak beers, can characteristically exhibit poor head retention. In general unmalted adjuncts, and roasted grains enhance head retention. Dark beers have better head retention than light coloured beers, etc. Try adding 5% to 10% brewers wheat flour to your grist makeup.

Beer does not clear properly.

Generally, a beer usually begins to clear towards the end of fermentation and the clearing process continues in the barrel or bottles. The cloudiness at this stage is mostly yeast in suspension, and the visible clearing is the yeast flocculating and rising to the surface, or sinking to the bottom of the vessel. A good strain of yeast will usually clear out of suspension unaided, leaving a crystal clear beer. However, some strains of yeast, working in certain types of beer, may not clear down quickly or may not clear down at all. Under these circumstances it is necessary to use finings. Isinglass is superior for removing yeast from suspension, but it may be ineffective against other haze forming particles. If isinglass is ineffective in solving the problem, then gelatine can be tried. Another cause of cloudy beer is poor filtration during the mash tun run-off, caused by allowing the bed of grain to crack during run-off or sparging. The same applies to the run-off after the boiling phase, where the hops are expected to filter out the trub.

Cloudiness and hazes

This paragraph mostly concerns hazes that form during storage, although some of the problems described can occur during fermentation. This is a difficult subject, there are a number of possible different causes of haze. As amateurs we are often not able to identify the cause of the problem.

Starch haze
A starch haze is caused by poor mashing technique, or to high a proportion of adjuncts in the grist makeup. You should always ensure that starch end point has been reached after mashing, before proceeding with the rest of the process. A starch haze can be identified by applying the starch end point test to the finished beer. The only cure is to add starch reducing enzymes to the finished beer, but it is not really worth it. If the beer tastes like beer, then drink it from a pewter tankard.

Protein haze

There will always be a certain amount of undegraded protein in the finished beer. This usually shows itself as a chill haze, that is, a haze which forms when the beer is cooled. However, an excess of undegraded protein can cause hazes to be formed at room temperature. Furthermore, protein-tannin complexes tend to come out of solution as beer ages. A protein haze can be identified to good probability by performing the starch end point test. If there is no starch present, and the beer tastes okay, then there is a fair chance that the haze is a protein haze. Treating the finished beer with bentonite, or, better still, a proper silica gel absorbant, will remove protein. A protein haze does not normally affect the taste of the finished beer, so again, another answer is to drink the beer from a pewter tankard. Excess protein is normally removed from the beer as trub during the boiling phase of beer production. For future brews, pay more attention to the boiling phase. Try employing a more vigorous boil, boil for longer, use Irish moss, and try forced cooling to remove more trub. Auxillary finings will help to remove protein, as will the addition of the protein reducing enzyme 'protease', but these should not really be necessary.

Yeast haze

A yeast haze can occur if the beer has been shaken; or if air has been admitted into solution during the racking process, causing the yeast to revert to aerobic respiration and multiplying. Strangely enough thunderstorms are known to cause a yeast haze. Usually the yeast will settle by itself. If the yeast does not settle within a few days, and no finings have been used, then the addition of isinglass finings will usually cure the problem. If isinglass finings have already been used, it will usually be sufficient to re-disperse the finings by rolling the barrel around, and then standing it on the stillage to settle.

Bacterial haze or sour beer

These two problems are related, apart from causing hazes, bacterial contamination can sour the beer. There really is no effective cure, it is better to discard the beer and tighten up on methods for future brews. Unlike brewer's yeast, most bacteria is either aerobic or anaerobic, they do not have the ability to switch from one form of respiration to the other. Aerobic bacteria are the most troublesome. This is because aerobic organisms are able to multiply very much faster than their anaerobic cousins, thereby establishing themselves very quickly. This is not to say that anaerobic organisms can not cause problems with beer, it is just that the beer is usually drunk before they have a chance to cause any problems.

As for tightening up procedures and methods; It goes without saying that absolute cleanliness, and proper sterilisation of anything that comes into contact with the beer, is of utmost importance. It is also important that from the initial fermentation stage, through to barrelling, the admission of oxygen into solution is avoided. This means using syphon tubes or transfer tubes that reach down to the bottom of the vessel being filled, the tube should be held below the surface of the liquid during filling. When filling barrels it is important to leave a minimum of headroom at the top of the barrel. A few hours after filling the barrel, the barrel should be carefully vented to expel the air. Air, being lighter than carbon dioxide, will be at the top of the barrel, with a layer of CO_2 being formed on the surface of the beer. Carefully venting the barrel in this way will expel the air in preference to the carbon dioxide. The addition of absorbic acid to the beer will reduce the dissolved oxygen content further. All of the common bacterial contaminants of beer are highly sensitive to sulphur dioxide. The addition of sodium metabisulphite to the finished beer as described in the chapter on finishing will keep almost all problematic bacteria in check.

Of the aerobic organisms that cause problems with beer, acetic acid bacteria is the most common. This causes the familiar off-taste when a landlord does not clean his pipes regularly. There are several different species of acetic acid bacteria, but all are sensitive to sulphur dioxide. Other aerobic bacteria include *Zymomanas*, producing hydrogen sulphide from dextrins, the well known 'Burton Stench'. *Eschericia coli, Enterobacter,* And *citrobacter* being other contaminants.

Of anaerobic bacteria, Lactic acid producers are the most common, again there are several species. Some of these apart from causing off-tastes and turbidity in beer, can also cause the beer to set into a thick jelly, cause a ropy effect in beer, cause an oily film on the beer, and 101 other things to happen. Many of these problems require a long time to take effect, but there is often sufficient time for problems to occur during the maturation of an old ale. Although the anaerobic lactic bacteria are slow to multiply, it does not take very long for their presence to be detected by an off-taste being formed. Lactic acid bacteria are highly sensitive to sulphur dioxide, but being anaerobic antioxidants such as absorbic acid are not effective.

20 Making Measurements

Temperature

There is not much that one can say about the measurement of temperature, everyone in the world must have used a thermometer at some time or another. However, there are a couple of precautions that should be taken when making very accurate measurements. The first of these is that all thermometers, whether conventional or electronic, are calibrated for a particular immersion depth. Some thermometers are calibrated for total immersion, while others are calibrated for partial immersion, say the first 75, 100, or 150 millimetres of the stem depending on type. All precision thermometers have the immersion depth engraved on them somewhere or indicated with a mark.

Another consideration is that the temperature of a mass is very rarely the same throughout its bulk. Heat rises, therefore most things will be hotter at the top than at the bottom. An insulated mash tun for instance loses its heat through the top and through the sides of the vessel, therefore its temperature will be greater in the middle than at the sides, and greater at the top than at the bottom. A wise precaution for accurate temperature measurement is to thoroughly stir the sample before taking the measurement or, where this is not possible, take several readings at different places and calculate an average. Fortunately, for the most part at least, brewing does not require very precise temperature measurements to be made.

Specific gravity

The specific gravity of a fluid is the ratio of its density in relation to the density of an identical volume of pure water at the same temperature. In other words the weight of the fluid to be measured, divided by the weight of an equal volume of pure water at the same temperature. Pure water has a specific gravity of 1.000, but if any substance is dissolved in the water the specific gravity will be altered. A fluid which has a specific gravity greater than 1 is heavier than water, whereas, a fluid which has a specific gravity less than 1 is lighter than water. A fluid which has a specific gravity of 1.050 will be 1.050 times heavier than the equivalent volume of pure water at the same temperature. In fact, at 20°C., 1 litre of this solution will weigh 1.050 kilograms, 50 grams heavier than 1 litre of pure water.

The specific gravity of a fluid is its weight, divided by the weight of an identical volume of pure water, thus:

$$S.G. = \frac{W_s}{W_w}$$

Alternatively: W_s = S.G. × W_w

Where: S.G. = Specific Gravity

W_s = Weight of sample to be measured

W_w = Weight of the same volume of pure water

Note: this assumes that both the sample and the water are at the same temperature

You may now be wondering why on earth we would wish to know the weight of our beer! Well, prior to fermentation any difference between the weight of our wort and the weight of an equivalent volume of water must be due to the materials we put into it, and any changes to the weight of our wort which take place during fermentation must be due to the fermentation process. Sugars are much heavier than water, thus, when the sugars which are extracted from our malt are dissolved in water, the density of the water and therefore its specific gravity is increased. On the other hand, alcohol is much lighter than water, thus, If alcohol is dissolved in water the specific gravity of the resultant solution is decreased. The specific gravity of our wort is not only a good guide to the strength and quality of our beer, but also enables us to keep a close check on the progress of fermentation. During fermentation heavy sugars in our wort are converted into carbon dioxide and alcohol. The carbon dioxide is given off to the atmosphere, but carbon dioxide does have weight, and the alcohol is lighter than water (ethyl alcohol has an s.g. 0.79044). The result is that during fermentation the density of our wort, hence its specific gravity decreases considerably.

Temperature effects

It is important to talk in terms of specific gravity and **not** in terms of weight, for although weight has been used in the descriptions above as a method of illustration, it is important to realise that specific gravity is **independent of temperature**, whereas the density of a fluid and therefore the weight of a given volume of fluid is **temperature dependent**. A fluid which has a specific gravity of 1.070 at 20°C will still have a specific gravity of 1.070 at 50°C. A fluid of s.g. 1.070 will weigh 1.070 times the weight of an equivalent volume of water at the same temperature irrespective of what the temperature or the absolute weight may be. It just so happens that at 20°C, **and only at 20°C**, 1 litre of this fluid will weigh 1.070 kilograms or 70 grams heavier than water. In fact at 50°C 1 litre of the same fluid will only be 59 grams heavier than 1 litre of water, but the density of water at 50°C has decreased proportionally, the ratio remains the same and the specific gravity is still 1.070.

Water expands with increasing temperature (usually). Beer, which is mostly water, expands at essentially the same rate. If we were to heat up 1 litre of water its volume would increase. The **total** quantity of water would weigh exactly the same as before, but, because that same weight occupies a greater volume, the density of the water and hence the weight of one litre will decrease.

This does not affect specific gravity because specific gravity is a **ratio** of two weights, our sample to be measured, and a reference standard – being the same volume of pure water at the same temperature as the sample. Specific gravity assumes that both the sample and the reference are at the same temperature. At other temperatures both the sample and the reference change density at the same rates, therefore the **ratio** of the two weights and hence our specific gravity remains essentially the same.

Brewerspeak

Part of the fascination of brewing is the industry's sense of individuality. Brewers have their own peculiar language, rather like modern computer buzz-words, but developed over centuries of usage. They have their own method of doing things, which is usually completely opposite to the way anyone else would do the same job. Brewers have their own unique units of measurement, which defy rational explanation. A quarter of barley is equivalent 448 lbs, but a quarter of malt is equivalent to 336 lbs! The traditional brewer's unit of measurement for specific gravity is brewers lbs per brewers barrel!

However, when the fancy takes them they do sometimes express specific gravity in terms which broadly resemble everyone else's terms, but being mindful of the great fun that can obtained by throwing the rest of the scientific world into complete confusion, they have characteristically adopted their own version of it. The most significant thing that brewers have done to s.g. is to multiply it by 1000, therefore s.g. 1.036 becomes 1036 in brewerspeak, s.g. 1.075 becomes 1075, and 1.0555 becomes 1055.5. Another change is that they have dropped the word 'specific' (brewers are very rarely specific about anything), therefore 'specific gravity' simply becomes 'gravity' in brewerspeak.

Then we have 'brewer's degrees' (they couldn't resist it), this is simply the practice of dropping the unimportant digits, or more correctly, subtracting 1000 from gravity. In brewers degrees, gravity 1075 is equivalent to 75 degrees, 1055.5 is 55.5 degrees, and etc. Easy ennit?.

The hydrometer

We could find the specific gravity of our wort by weighing it and comparing it against the weight of the same volume of pure water. However, such methods are clumsy and impractical from our point of view. Fortunately there is a much simpler method, and that is by the use of a simple and inexpensive instrument called a hydrometer. The hydrometer is simply a calibrated glass tube, which is weighted to float at a particular depth in water. The level to which the hydrometer will sink in fluids is dependent upon the density of that fluid. The hydrometer carries a scale, calibrated in specific gravity, which indicates the depth to which it will sink when immersed in fluids of differing densities. One simply dunks the instrument into the fluid to be measured and reads the specific gravity directly from the scale.

Using the hydrometer

A certain amount of care is required in the use of the hydrometer if accurate results are to be obtained. The first precaution is to ensure that both the hydrometer and the sample jar are quite clean and sterile, if you are going to return the sample to the beer. The usual measurement procedure is to draw off a sample of the wort to be measured into a sample jar, and then to stand the jar onto a level surface. Carefully lower the hydrometer into the sample. Spin the hydrometer in the sample to ensure that it is properly wetted and to dislodge any bubbles that may be clinging to the sides of the instrument. As soon as the hydrometer is stationary, ensure that it is not touching the sides of the jar, and then carefully read the specific gravity directly from the scale. The measurment should be performed quickly because bubbles will begin to cling to the side of the instrument, causing the hydrometer to slowly rise, giving an incorrect reading as a result.

Surface tension causes a meniscus to be present on the surface of the sample. Care must be exercised to ensure that the reading is taken where the lower surface of the liquid intersects the scale and NOT at the top of the meniscus. The reading should always be taken at eye level to eliminate any errors caused by diffraction through the fluid.

Temperature correction

Yes there had to be a snag! The hydrometer should really be called a densitometer because **it actually measures density,** it is merely **calibrated** in terms of specific gravity **(relative density)**. This is unfortunate because the absolute density of a fluid changes with temperature, whereas relative density or specific gravity does not. This means that the hydrometer can only give accurate results at one temperature, the temperature for which it is calibrated. Hydrometers intended for brewing use are usually calibrated for 15 or 16°C which is a typical fermentation temperature, whereas hydrometers intended for chemistry are usually calibrated for 20°C. At temperatures other than the calibration temperature the hydrometer gives the wrong specific gravity indication. Fortunately the variation of the density of water with temperature is accurately known, and by the use of a correction table we are able to adjust our indicated gravity to find the true gravity. However, one should not attempt to measure specific gravity at high temperatures because the measurement errors will become greater at higher temperatures. When measuring the specific gravity of the mash, or of the wort from the copper, the sample should be cooled to a sensible temperature before making the measurement. Cooling can be achieved

TABLE 20.1
HYDROMETER TEMPERATURE CORRECTION TABLE

Hydrometer calibration 3°C — C.F.	20°C	15°C temperature	60°F	C.F.
−2				−2
10°C	5°C		40°F	
−1				−1
	18°C	13°C	55°F	
0				0
	22°C	18°C	67°F	
+1				+1
	26°C	23°C	75°F	
+2				+2
29°C	27°C		81°F	
+3				+3
	32°C	30°C	87°F	
+4				+4
	35°C	33°C	93°F	
+5				+5
	38°C	36°C	97°F	
+6				+6
	41°C	39°C	103°F	
+7				+7
	43°C	41°C	107°F	
+8				+8
	46°C	44°C	111°F	
+9				+9
	48°C	46°C	114°F	
+10				+10
	50°C	48°C	119°F	

(Left margin vertical label: Correction Factor)

by standing the sample jar in cold water, or by running tap water over the sides of the jar — taking care to ensure than none of the water gets inside the jar! Below, you will find a temperature correction table for hydrometers calibrated at 15°C, 20°C and 60°F, be sure to use the correct one for your hydrometer. At low temperatures, particularly if close to the calibration temperature, the errors are small enough to be ignored for most practical purposes.

Using the table

The table is suitable for hydrometers that are calibrated at 60°F, 15°C, or 20°C by using the appropriate temperature column. The correction factor is in the extreme left hand and extreme right hand columns. Observe that the correction factor is offset from the temperature columns, lying between two temperatures. From the table, for a hydrometer calibrated at 15°C, the correction factor is $+3$ for wort temperatures betwwen 29°C and 32°C. and $+8$ for wort temperatures between 41°C and 44°C. The correction factor is added or subtracted from the indicated gravity as appropriate.

Example
If a sample of wort has a temperature of 30°C and an indicated gravity of 1042 using a 20°C hydrometer;
   From the table, the correction factor at 30°C $= +3$.
   Therefore true gravity $= 1042 +3 = 1045$

Starch end point test

This is a most useful test which is applied to the sweet wort during mashing. The starch end point test is used to ensure that all of the starch contained in the malt has been converted into maltose. This is important because, not only would an excess of starch indicate an inefficient or incomplete conversion, but its presence will also cause a protein haze in the finished beer. The starch end point test is both simple and accurate, the reagent used is iodine. Simply place a teaspoon of the mashed grain and sweet wort onto a white tile or saucer. Onto this, run a few drops of domestic iodine, or a proper iodine starch indicator after giving the indicator a good shake. If the mixture turns a deep blue — black, starch is still present, if the mixture stays the same colour, starch is not present. Although domestic iodine will work perfectly well as an indicator, it is better to order, or arrange your local chemist to make a proper iodine blue solution. This is an iodine solution containing a stabiliser and an indicator, usually a mixture of iodine and potassium iodide. The reason for this is that the solution is standardised and of known good performance, and the colour change is not so easily masked by wort colour.

Acidity measurement

The enzymes responsible for all of the major happenings that take place during the brewing process are sensitive to the acidity of the solution in which they are working. These enzymes work most efficiently at a particular acidity. The acidity of the mash is quite important, particularly as regards consistency and repeatability, also, the acidity of the wort prior to fermentation is important for fast, healthy yeast growth.

Acidity can be expressed in various ways, it can be expressed in parts per 1000 of the constituent acid, it can be expressed in the standard form of parts per 1000 – normalised in terms of sulphuric acid, or it can be expressed in terms of hydrogen ion content – pH.

By far the most convenient method, as regards brewing, is in terms of hydrogen ion content (pH).

pH (hydrogen ion content)

pH is the logarithm of the hydrogen ion content of a solution, and is a measure of the acidity or alkalinity of that solution. The pH scale runs from 0 to 14, where 0 is maximum acidity, 7 is neutrality, and 14 is maximum alkalinity. A pH figure of less than 7 is acid, and a pH above 7 is alkaline. The pH scale is logarithmic, a pH of 4 is ten times more acid than a pH of 5. A pH of 5.3 is twice as acid as a pH of 5.6. It is, however, important to realise that acidity and pH are not quite the same thing. They are related but not equivalent.

Measurement of pH

Electronic pH meters are available, but these are rather expensive. The easiest way for the amateur to measure pH is by means of indicator papers. These are supplied as booklets of fifty or so papers, and should be available from your local home brew shop. Indicator papers which cover a range of pH4 to pH6 are most suitable. The indicator papers change colour depending upon the pH of the solution into which they are dipped. Simply dunk an indicator paper into the solution to be tested and compare it, against a white background, with the colour scale supplied. A saucer or a tile makes a suitable white background.

Measuring small quantities.

In the domestic environment we do not have the facilities for measuring very small quantities of fluids or powder. Weighing things in small amounts is particularly difficult. This is not normally a problem with such things as cleaning or sterilising solutions where we simply need to ensure that the stuff is strong enough to perform the job; making a too strong a solution is unlikely to do any harm.

However, it is a problem if we wish too make up a solution of something to be added to the beer, where making too weak a solution would not have the desired effect, and making too strong a solution would be harmful in one way or another.

One way of overcoming the problem is to make up our solutions in much larger volumes, which we are able to measure using domestic equipment, and either storing the surplus as a standard solution, or throwing it away. A standard solution so derived can then be used

Measuring fluids in small volumes is easier than trying to weigh powders. Measuring small volumes of a fluid is easily achieved by using a graduated syringe. Cheap plastic graduated syringes are available in various sizes, your local chemist should be able to help. Chemists also stock calibrated dose spoons for medicines, these are also useful to the home brewer.

The acquisition of one or more professional glass measuring cylinders would be a very worthwhile investment. A 250 ml measuring cylinder will double as a hydrometer trial jar, whereas other sizes, from say 100 ml down to about 10 ml are useful for accurately measuring critical substances to be added to beer such as hop extracts, hop oils, sulphite, primings, finings, etc. Measuring cylinders are expensive, and are not likely to be found in your local high street, but the science department of your local college, or a local school will probably be prepared to obtain them for you.

Sodium metabisulphite

Sodium metabisulphite releases sulphur dioxide when in solution. Many forms of bacteria are killed by sulphur dioxide, whereas brewers yeast is unaffected by low concentrations. Thus, sodium metabisulphite can be added to beer in low concentrations as a stabiliser to keep infecting organisms at bay, while allowing the yeast to continue to work and produce secondary condition. Furthermore, sodium metabisulphite is an antioxidant which retards any oxidation processes that takes place in beer. It also serves to stabilise absorbic acid (vitamin C; another antioxidant) in solution, and is therefore useful as a stabiliser when absorbic acid is added to beer.

When sodium metabisulphite is used in high concentrations as a steriliser for cleaning utensils etc, accurate measurement is not important. However, when it is added to beer in low concentrations as a stabiliser, accurate measurement is essential. Too low a level, and it will not have the desired effect; too high a level and the taste of sulphur may be detected in the beer; at even higher concentrations the yeast itself may be killed.

A maximum concentration of sodium metabisulphite in beer when used as a stabiliser is 110 milligrams per litre (110 parts per million), which equates to 70ppm of sulphur dioxide in solution. Obviously, there is no way that we can weigh to such limits in the domestic environment; weighing tens of grams is difficult enough without having to contend with milligrams (1000th of a gram). We overcome the measurement problem by making up a standard high strength solution, using quantities that we are able to measure, and then, if necessary, diluting this solution even further until the desired strength is reached.

The home brewing and home wine making world seems to have settled upon a 10% stock solution of sodium metabisulphite; and this is made up as follows:

10% STOCK SOLUTION

2oz of Sod. met.   made up to: 1 pint with water

OR:
50g of Sod. met.   500 ml with water

OR:
100g of Sod. met.   1 litre with water

'Made up to' means put the powder into the measuring vessel first and *add* the water until the specified volume is reached. That way we have a known volume containing a known quantity of powder. Deionised or distilled water should be used if available because the solution will remain stable under storage for a longer period of time. However, tap water can be used if deionised water is not available.

The resulting solution can be used 'neat' as a steriliser or, with further dilution as specified below, as a stabiliser for adding to beer. The solution will gradually deteriorate over a period of time, but will be usable for a period of about three months as a stabiliser, but much longer if only used as a steriliser.

Unfortunately the amount of free sulphur dioxide provided by a given solution of sodium metabisulphite is dependent upon the assay value (purity) of the sodium metabisulphite used. Thus, even with the most careful measurements, our level of released free sulphur dioxide will be somewhat approximate. The assay value is not the sort of information that is usually provided on a home – brew package. An assay value of 95% is the maximum purity that we are likely to be using, therefore, an assay value of 95% is assumed in the following calculations; which is near enough for our purposes.

A 10% stock solution will contain 100 grams per litre of sodium metabisulphite, which, at 95% assay, will provide 64 grams per litre (64000 ppm) of free sulphur dioxide.

5ml (1 teaspoonful) of this solution in 1 gallon (4.55 litres) of water or beer will provide 0.32 grams of sulphur dioxide which equates to 70ppm. Therefore, five teaspoons of 10% stock solution in a five gallon batch of beer will provide the maximum dose rate of 70ppm. The use of sodium metabisulphite of lower assay value than 95% will provide correspondingly lower levels of sulphur dioxide, but, in any case, it is not likely to be any lower than 60ppm under the above conditions.

The following table gives the amount of sulphur dioxide, in parts per million, provided by adding a quantity of 10% stock solution to a given volume of fluid.

TABLE 20.2

10% stk (ml)	1 pt.	1 ltr	1 gal	5gals	25ltrs
		Volume of fluid added to			
1	112	64	14	2.8	2.5
2	224	127	28	5.6	5
3	336	191	42	8.4	7.5
4	448	255	56	11.2	10
5	560	318	70	14	12.5
10	1128	636	141	28	25
15		955	211	42	37.5
20		1273	282	56	50
25			352	70	62.5
30			422	84	75

Concentration of SO_2 in parts per million

Campden tablets

Tablets are an easy and accurate method of measuring small quantities of a solid; albeit an expensive method of purchasing the substance concerned.

Campden tablets are a steriliser, originally devised for fruit preserving; are based on either sodium metabisulphite, or potassium metabisulphite and are a source of sulphur dioxide. Campden tablets are made by a number of manufacturers in various different weights and compositions.

The amount of free sulphur dioxide produced depends upon the composition of the tablet, and of course, the assay value of the materials used. Campden tablets based upon sodium metabisulphite will produce about 64% sulphur dioxide; therefore one 0.5 gram tablet will be equivalent to 5ml or one teaspoonful of our 10% stock solution described above. However, Campden tablets based upon potassium metabisulphite will produce only 53% sulphur dioxide, so an adjustment may need to be made if this form of Campden tablet is purchased.

In general, 5 to 6 Campden tablets per five gallon batch of beer will suffice to stabilise it against infection, whereas the same amount in half a litre of water will serve as a sterilising solution.

Sugar solutions

If we take 1 litre of water and add 200 grams of sugar to it, the resulting solution will have a specific gravity of 1.066, which means that, at 20°C, **1 litre** of this solution is 66 grams heavier than water. This simple statement often causes some confusion among novice brewers who naturally wonder where on earth the other 134 grams went! The confusion is further compounded when one states that the actual sugar content of the same solution is 177 grams per litre!

The reason why the addition of 200 grams of sugar to one litre of water produces a sugar content of only 177 grams per litre, is, of course, because the addition of the sugar increases the volume (from 1 litre to 1.126 litres). The specific volume of white household sugar is about 0.63 l/kg, this means that the addition of 1 kilogram of sugar to a volume of water will increase the total volume by 0.63 of a litre or 630 millilitres. In the case of our example above:

New volume = old volume + (weight of sugar x 0.63)

$$= 1+(0.200 \times 0.63) = 1+(0.126) = 1.126 \; litres$$

We can calculate our specific gravity directly from the new volume if we desired, thus:

$$Specific \; gravity \; = \frac{W_s}{W_w} = \frac{1.200}{1.126} = 1.0657$$

We can calculate the amount of dissolved sugar per litre by dividing the amount of added sugar by the new volume. Thus:

$$Dissolved \; sugar = \frac{200g}{1.126} = 177 \; grams \; per \; litre$$

We are now able to see where 23 grams of our missing sugar went, but there are still 111 grams unaccounted for! The secret to this little poser is the simple fact that if we have 177 grams of sugar in our 1 litre of solution, it must have replaced (displaced) its equivalent volume of water! To arrive at our true increase in weight, we should subtract the weight of the water thus displaced, from the weight of the added sugar. As I mentioned earlier, the specific volume of household sugar is about 0.63 l/kg. If we multiply 177 × 0.63 we get the volume of water which was displaced by the sugar,

177g × 0.63 = 111 ml (one of our magic figures)

Now; 111 millilitres of pure water at 20°C weighs exactly 111 grams, thus:

177g — 111g = 66 grams (another magic figure)

66 grams, gives us an s.g. of 1.066.

Weights and measures

One domestic (5ml) teaspoon holds the following approximate weights of the specified substances:

Absorbic acid	1.5g
Ammonium phosphate	5g
Calcium carbonate	3g
Citric acid	4g
Granulated sugar	6g
Irish moss	3g
Sodium bicarbonate	5.5g
Sodium metabisuphite	6g
Sodium hydroxide	7g

A domestic teaspoon holds approximately: 5 ml.
A domestic desert spoon holds approximately: 9ml.
A domestic tablespoon holds approximately: 15ml.
A large coffee mug holds approximately: 300ml.

To convert:

Ounces to grams	Multiply by: 28.3495
Pounds to kilograms	Multiply by: 0.453592
Pints to litres	Multiply by: 0.557
Gallons to litres	Multiply by: 4.456

To convert the other way, divide by the figure shown.

1 cubic metre	= 33.315 cu ft.
	= 219.98 Imperial gallons
	= 1000 litres
	= 10hl
1 Imp. gallon	= 160 fluid ounces
1 cubic foot	= 6.25 Imperial gallons
1 lb per gallon	= 99.76 grams per litre
1 brewer's barrel	= 36 gallons
1 brewer's quarter of barley	= 448 lb
1 brewer's quarter of malt	= 336 lb

Glossary of terms

Acrospire: The small shoot which grows out of the barley during germination.

Adjunct: The term applied to grain added to the **grist** which draws upon enzymes supplied by malt to effect the conversion of starch into sugar. A material which does not draw upon these enzymes is not strictly speaking an adjunct.

Aerobic respiration: In our case, refers to the respiration of yeast (or bacteria) utilising air. Provides rapid yeast growth, but little alcohol is produced.

Ale: A malt beverage fermented by a top working yeast.

Alpha acid: The hop resin humulon. A measure of the principle bittering substances contained in hops.

Alcohol: In the brewing context refers to ethanol (ethyl alcochol).

Alhpa amylase: See Amylase.

Amino acid: Low order nitrogenous substances, required by the yeast for growth.

Amylase: Alpha-amylase and Beta-amylase are the enzymes responsible for the conversion on starch into sugars during the mash. Often refered to collectively as **diastase**.

Anaerobic repiration: In our case, refers to a form of respiration, of yeast (or bacteria), which does not require the presence of air. Alcoholic fermentation by our yeast is only performed under anaerobic conditions.

Armstrong rake: A rotating arm fitted to the bottom of the mash tun for mixing the **grist** with the **liquor** prior to **mashing**, also used for loosening the mash should it set firm. More commonly called a **porcupine**.

Attemperator: Pipes set inside the fermentation vessel, through which hot or cold water can be pumped to control the temperature of fermentation.

Attenuation: The drop in specific gravity of the **wort** during the process of fermentation.

Autolysis: When a yeast dies, it is digested by its own enzyme system.

Auxiliary finings: Finings which are sometimes used in conjunction with **isinglass** under special circumstances.

Back: Pronounced 'buck'. Brewerspeak for a holding vessel. From the same etymology as the modern word bucket.

Balm: pronounced 'barm'. Old Brewerspeak for yeast.

Barrel: A 36 gallon cask. Brewers standard unit of measurement.

Barley wine: A strong ale.

Batch fermentation: The traditional method of brewing ale in individual batches.

Beer: Generic term for malt beverages. Nowadays the term is used interchangably with ale, and sometimes refers to weak ales.

Beta acid: The hop resin lupulon.

Beta glucan: A gummy substance found in the aleurone layer of barley.

Unmalted grains are rich in these gums. In moderation beta glucan aids beer foaming, but an excess could cause mash tun run-off problems.

Bottom fermentation: Bottom working refers to fermentation by a yeast which sits on the bottom of the fermentation vessel. Typical of lager yeasts.

Burtonising: Brewerspeak for the act of water treatment, historically was the act of making the water similar to that of Burton upon Trent by adding **calcium sulphate**.

Calcium bicarbonate: The principle substance causing temporary hardness in our water supplies. A substantial quantity can be precipitated by boiling the water for a short period.

Calcium Sulphate: The principle substance causing permanent hardness in our water supplies. Can not be removed by boiling.

Cask: General term for all draught beer containers.

Cask conditioned beer: Beer which conditions in the cask rather than in conditioning tanks at the brewery.

Casting: The act of emptying a vessel.

Cereals: Grain such as wheat, barley, or maize; used as malt adjuncts.

Chitting: A term used to describe the initial growth of barley during malting.

Cistern: In a traditional maltings, is the vessel in which the barley is steeped in water.

Conditioning: Maturation of beer after it leaves the fermenter.

Copper: The vessel in which the wort is boiled prior to fermentation. refered to in the north of England as a **kettle**

Copper finings: A substance, usually **Irish moss**, added to the copper during the boil to aid the protein break and improve the stability of the finished beer.

Cracking: The act of lightly crushing grain in order to expose the **endosperm** to the **liquor** during mashing.

Dextrins: The term given to non fermentable and slowly fermentable sugars remaining in the **wort** after fermentation, they provide residual sweetness and body.

Diastase: Old fashioned collective name given to **amylase** group enzymes responsible for the conversion of starch into sugar during the mash.

D.M.S.: Diastatic Malt Syrup, a malt extract that has a high level of enzymic activity and can be used to assist the conversion of **adjuncts** during a mash.

Dropping: In a brewery, is the act of transfering a fluid by the influence of gravity into another vessel, usually situated on the floor below.

Dropping system: A brewing method whereby the fermenting wort is **dropped** into a secondary vessel about half way through fermentation, leaving **trub**, hop debris, and surplus yeast behind.

Dry hopping: The act of adding a few hop cones to the beer after barelling to add 'hoppy' aroma.

Endosperm: The starch rich centre of the barley grain.

Enzyme: A biological form of catalyst.

Fining: The practice of speeding or aiding the clearing of beer by adding colloidial, or alginate type substances.

Finishing: Post fermentation processes.

Firkin: A 9 gallon cask.

Flocculation: The ability of yeast to rise to the surface of the **wort** during and after the process of fermentation.

Gelatine: A colloid derived from animal hooves, used as a fining agent in home brewing.

Glycolysis: The act of sugar being broken down into its component parts during fermentation.

Glycoprotein: Protein with carbohydrate links, derived from the barley. Unmalted grains are rich in glycoprotein. Assists head retention.

Goods: In brewerspeak, **grist** becomes **goods** when it is mixed with water in the **mash tun**.

Green beer: Beer that has not yet **matured**

Green malt: Malt that has not been kilned.

Grains: Brewerspeak for spent **goods**.

Grist: The mixture of milled malt and **adjuncts** waiting for the mash tun.

Grits: Raw cereals which have been milled to remove the aleurone layer. Grits do not find favour in British brewing practice. Most grits need to be cooked before mashing.

Gyle: A particular brew or batch of beer.

Hogshead: A 54 gallon cask.

Hop back: In a brewery, the vessel into which the wort is run after boiling to allow the spent hops and **trub** to settle, trub is filtered out by the spent hops acting as a filter bed on the perforated floor.

Hop extract: Essential substances extracted from hops in a factory. Used extensively in home brewing to eliminate a hop boil.

Hot break: The point at which the undesirable protein in the wort begins to precipitate out of solution during boiling.

Initial heat: The temperature at which **mashing** begins.

Invert sugar: The form of sucrose that breweries prefer to use, it is ready inverted into its component parts of fructose and glucose, which saves the yeast having to do it. Brewers feel that invert sugar is not as prone to causing hangovers as is non inverted sucrose.

Isinglass: A rather mysterious **fining** agent.

Iso-acids: The essential bittering substances of hops in a water soluble form.

Kilderkin: An 18 gallon cask.

Krausening: The practice of using **wort** as a priming agent rather than priming sugars.

Lintner: A unit of measure of the diastatic power of a malt.

Liquor: Brewerspeak for brewing water.

Maltose: Malt sugar

Malt extract: A syrup that can be used as a short cut method of brewing, ideal for beginners.

Mashing: The process of extracting fermentable sugars from malted grain.

Maturation: A period of time which should be allowed for the proper flavour of the beer to develop.

Milling: See **cracking**.

Original gravity: The gravity at which fermentation is begun.

Paraflow: The common name for a brewery plate heat exchanger type of wort cooler, actually a registered trade mark.

Peptide: The intermediate stage between a protein and an amino acid. It is produced by the enzyme peptidase.

Ph: A measure of the hydrogen ion content, and hence the acidity of a fluid.

Pin: A 4.5 gallon cask.

Pitching: The act of introducing yeast into the fermentation vessel.

Polyphenol: A complex group of compounds found in beer. They react with other components in the beer and influence beer colour, haze, and head retention. They also assist the **hot break** in the wort boil.

Porcupine: See **Armstrong rake**.

Priming: The act of adding sugar or wort to the barrels, to provide secondary fermentation and condition.

Rack: Brewerspeak for transfering a fluid leaving sediment behind. ie, filling barrels with beer.

Racking back: Brewerspeak for the open tank in which **green beer** is held for a short period before being transfered to the barrels.

Racking gravity: The specific gravity at which the **green beer** is put into barrels or bottles, usually a few degrees higher than **final gravity**.

Refrigerator: Common name for a simple cold water based brewery wort cooler, not true refrigeration in the modern sense of the word.

Retorrification: The act of warming the **grist** prior to **mashing** in order to reduce the differential between **strike heat** and **initial heat**.

Rousing: The act of stirring yeast into the beer in order to keep it in suspension. Sometimes refers to aerating the wort to maintain yeast activity.

Run off: The act of emptying a vessel, usually the mash tun.

Saccharification: The conversion of starch into sugar by the means of enzymes.

Secondary fermentation: Process by which beer continues to slowly ferment and mature during conditioning.

Shive: Wooden bung with a penetrable centre core, fitted to beer casks. A porous wooden peg (spile) is driven through the centre to vent the cask.

Skimming: The act of removing surplus yeast from the surface of the wort during fermentation.

Sparging: The act of flushing valuable sugars from the **goods** in the mash tun.

Sparge arm: A rotating perforated pipe which sprays hot **liquor** over the **goods** during **sparging**. Behaves like a rotory lawn sprinkler.

Sparkler: Adjustable nozzle fitted to a beer pump. It is used to control the amount of head on a pint.

Spile: A wooden peg which is knocked through a shive on a cask.

Steeping: Exposure of barley to water prior to malting.

Stillage: A brick, wooden, or metal structure which supports casks of beer in the pub cellar.

Square: A vessel.

Strike heat: The temperature at which the mash **liquor** is maintained prior to the **grist** being added.

Sweet wort: The wort as collected from the mash tun before being boiled.

Trub: Undesirable protein matter precipitated during the boil.

Trumpet: Brewerspeak for funnel shaped devices.

Tunner: Brewerspeak for a spraying rose.

Ullage: The empty space in a cask.

Underback: A heated vessel used to collect the runnings from the mash tun in readiness for the boil.

Underletting: The practice of running hot water into the bottom of the mash tun to raise the temperature of the mash if it drops too low.

Venting: The act of allowing excess carbon dioxide to escape from a cask of beer prior to serving.

Wort: Pronounced 'wurt'. The sugary fluid which is extracted from our malt and fermented by our yeast.

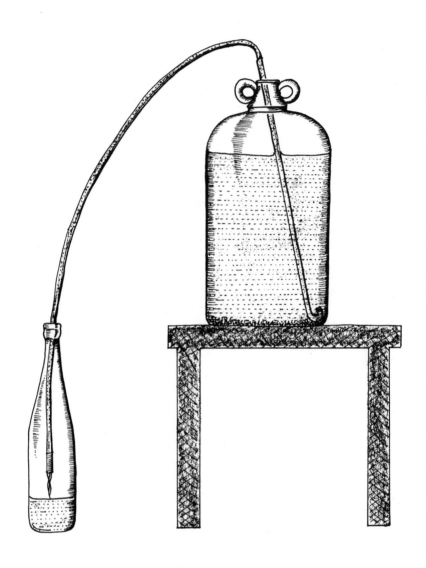

Racking into a bottle

INDEX

"...if I'd a knowed what a trouble it was to make a book I wouldn't a tackled it and aint agoing to no more."
(Mark Twain, Adventures of Hucklberry Finn, 1885.)